Educational Project Management

DESMOND L. COOK

*Director of the Educational
Program Management Center
The Ohio State University*

Charles E. Merrill Publishing Company
A Bell & Howell Company
Columbus, Ohio

International Standard Book Number: 0-675-09271-X

Library of Congress Catalog Card Number: 70-134431

1 2 3 4 5 6 7 8 9 10–75 74 73 72 71

Printed in the United States of America

Foreword

Educational Project Management breaks new ground in providing a comprehensive view of the science of project management as it relates to the field of educational research and development. Written by the man most responsible for introducing applications of the PERT management and planning system to educational situations, the book sets forth the basic functions of project management, the role of the project manager, and the organizational implications of project management. It delineates decision-making procedures to assure that complex research, development, and demonstration programs will be carried to their conclusion within time and cost estimates and against established performance criteria, and provides illustrations from the educational scene.

The application of sophisticated project management techniques in the applied social sciences is a relatively recent phenomenon. And, as management can be credited for the successes in fields such as space exploration and industrial development, so too increasingly sophisticated management is required for large-scale programs of research, development, and demonstration in education. As the process of reaching program objectives becomes more complex, the need for scientific management grows correspondingly. A project with a budget of a few thousand dollars and a staff of one or two hardly poses the same management requirements as a million-dollar development program whose success depends on efficient schedules, precise relationships among pieces of work, many individuals, and appropriate allocations of money.

Educational historians may someday call ours the *Age of Accountability*. Both our educational institutions and those engaged in educational research, development, and demonstration are being challenged —the schools, to be accountable for children's learning, the R&D enterprise, to be accountable for projects whose success is defined in terms of impact on school practice. The development of management sophistication among educators can help us meet these demands. Educational managers, professionals, and professionals-turned-managers will find this book of value in setting forth procedures and principles that will enhance their performance and their ability to meet their commitments—in short, their accountability. Similarly, the book will also assist managers in agencies which fund such projects. The strategies it presents are as relevant to the management of a large government funding program as they are to the actual conduct of those programs.

Although the necessity for competent management is part of the conventional wisdom of business and industry, the concept of educator as manager or researcher as manager is just being accepted—gingerly. Although educators and researchers may indeed have *functioned* as managers—manipulating resources and coping with multiple demands to meet certain ends—the tools devised by managers in other fields have not been available to them, nor has the relevance of such tools been immediately evident. This book brings both the perspective and the tools of sound management to the attention of educators and of researchers, it demonstrates their relevance, and finally, it brings them into service.

Howard J. Hjelm

Acting Associate Commissioner
National Center for Educational
*   Research and Development*
U.S. Office of Education
Washington, D.C.

Preface

The preparation of this work was undertaken as a direct experience in the management of funded research and development projects in the field of education, along with a developing interest in the application of management and management science concepts to educational situations. It is hoped that by passing on to the educational community the benefits of this experience and study others will find the way easier as they are called upon to plan and implement educational projects.

Several reasons could be advanced as to why persons having responsibility for the conduct of projects in the field of education should have an interest in the general concept of project management. While perhaps identifiable as somewhat separate reasons, there is an integrating theme which helps to justify the general content of this book. *This theme is the rapid development of the so-called project approach to dealing with educational problems.*

The increased presence of projects, usually of a research or development nature, in a college or university, state department of education, or a local school district has stemmed largely from the increased availability of funds to conduct such projects. Several notable pieces of legislation by the federal government during the past decade have provided a wide variety of funds available. The Cooperative Research Program of 1956 was probably the initial major act to provide funds for specific projects. This act was followed by the National Defense Education Act of 1958 which also provided funds for a wide variety of educational programs and projects, including curriculum development topics, guidance and counseling programs, media programs and the like. The Vocational Education Act of 1963 provided large amounts of funds for a wide variety of projects and programs related to the general field of vocational and technical education. The above three acts, while having some strong impact on the field of education, were soon to be overshadowed by the Elementary and Secondary Education Act of 1965. This act with its several titles provided a wide source of funding for projects dealing with education problems at all levels. Among its features were funds to increase the research competency of persons associated with the various activities funded under the program as well as the establishment of research and development centers, regional educational laboratories, and similar ventures.

One significant aspect of the increased financing and the availability of funds for support of educational projects is that the projects have become much larger in terms of the scope of the work to be done, the number of personnel involved, the size of the budget, and the duration of the study. This change in education is almost as great as the change from the corner grocery store to the supermarket operation in the food industry. It is now not extraordinary to find programs and projects exceeding $2,000,000 in budget with staffs of thirty to fifty professional persons, and running for a period of five to ten years.

The success of such projects may depend as much upon the management skills of the person placed in charge as upon his technical skills or substantative knowledge in the area under investigation. It is therefore important that educators become highly familiar with management concepts and principles as they carry out their assigned tasks. Unfortunately, it has been the author's observation that many persons placed in charge of projects lack the necessary management background to plan and control the effort adequately. This book has been written as an attempt to bring together some basic ideas and working suggestions to help alleviate this problem until more formal training can be provided to persons through colleges, universities, inservice programs, and other means.

The techniques presented in the book are considered to be general in nature, but some emphasis has been given to network-based management systems for project planning and control. This is a purposeful choice since it is felt that these types of systems hold the most potential for the project manager in the field of education. Such techniques were developed in situations in the government, the military, and industry analogous to those in which educational personnel most often find themselves.

The materials presented in the book have been assisted in their development through the funding of projects to the author by the U. S. Office of Education. The initial work was a study on PERT applications in education which resulted in a Cooperative Research Program Monograph entitled *PERT: Applications in Education* distributed through the U. S. Government Printing Office. Subsequent funding for conducting a series of management training programs for educational personnel provided an opportunity to secure reaction to the ideas, their organization, and the further refinement of materials. The concepts and ideas have undergone trial in the author's course on Research Management in the College of Education at Ohio State University. These experiences resulted in revision of materials in order to clarify the ideas for presentation in this book.

In addition to these experiences, it has been the author's good fortune to have attended seminars on management concepts presented by Kepner-Tregoe Associates, an advanced project planning and control sponsored by CEIR, Inc., a training course on management information systems sponsored by the PERT Orientation and Training Center operated by the Department of Defense, and a summer course on management information systems conducted by UCLA.

It would be completely inappropriate to state that all of the ideas are mine alone. The concepts, ideas, and practices presented herein have been drawn from attendance at formal courses on management, conversations with management specialists, reading, and the lessons learned from the actual management of research and development efforts. In addition, experiences gained from consultations with and/or the conduct of training programs for federal, state, and local school districts have broadened the base for ideas and practical suggestions.

D. L. C.

Acknowledgements

This book represents the output of many persons. To acknowledge the contributions of all would be a difficult task. The author would particularly like to acknowledge the initial encouragement provided by Dr. Howard Hjelm of the U. S. Office of Education and Dr. David L. Clark, currently Dean of the College of Education at Indiana University, when work was started in this area. Without the time, facilities, and moral support provided by Dr. Egon G. Guba in his role as Director of the Bureau of Educational Research and Service at Ohio State University, until that office was dissolved, the exploration into project management might not have been possible. A deep debt of gratitude is owed to several colleagues and graduate students who have assisted the author in collecting materials and acting as sounding boards for ideas. Among such persons were JoAnn King, Earl Stahl, William Loeber, Duane Dillman, and Steve Gyuro.

It would be a very strong injustice if acknowledgement was not made to the literally hundreds of students and colleagues around the country and abroad who have listened to the author discuss the concept of project management. Their questions, comments, and suggestions were of immense value in framing the contents of this publication.

Preliminary drafts of materials in the chapters have been prepared during the past couple of years by Polly Baun and Sue Metzmaier. The typing of the preliminary complete draft and final versions of the total manuscript was done by Penny King. Her humor and attitude toward the task was of immense value in helping the author through the task of writing and editing. Jeff Gore of Ohio State University prepared the illustrations and charts for the manuscript. His assistance in this area was of great value.

A debt beyond repayment is owed to my wife, Helen-Louise, for her patience and understanding regarding my need to write this book. She has spent many evenings alone while the author has been on the road. Perhaps this book can be a small taken of repayment for those many lonely evenings.

D. L. C.

For

Honey, Dave, and Bob

Shakespeare on Project Management

When we mean to build,
We first survey the plot, then draw the model.
And when we see the figure of the house,
Then must we rate the cost of the erection,
Which if we find outweighs ability,
What do we then but draw anew the model
In fewer offices, or at least desist
To build at all? Much more, in this great work,
Which is almost to pluck a kingdom down
And set another up, should we survey
The plot of situation and the model,
Consent upon a sure foundation,
Question surveyors, know our own estate,
How able such a work to undergo,
To weigh against his opposite. Or else
We fortify in paper and in figures,
Using the names of men instead of men,
Like one that draws the model of a house
Beyond his power to build it, who, half through,
Gives o'er and leaves his part-created cost
A naked subject to the weeping clouds
And waste for churlish winter's tyranny.

Henry IV
Part II, Act I, Scene III

TABLE OF CONTENTS

part **1**

Projects and Their Relationship to Management

This section will introduce the reader to the concept of project management and the emerging role of the project manager. Since this position requires a knowledge of general management functions and processes, the elementary concepts and principles of these topics are presented here. The section concludes with consideration of the various types of management systems which have evolved to assist the project manager in carrying out his duties and responsibilities.

chapter **1**

The Nature of Project Management

The role of a project manager, also referred to as a project director or a principal investigator, is relatively new, not only in the field of education but also in other areas, such as the military, government, and business. No specific point in time marks the introduction of this role. It has emerged gradually in the last two decades as a consequence of increased mission-oriented activities which, in a large part, have been supported by federal funds. Consequently, there has been a rising concern about the role of the project manager, and an equal concern about the more general concept of project management. This chapter will discuss the general concept of project management. It will present the characteristics of projects, discuss the general approaches to the placement of projects in organizations, outline some of the problems faced by the project manager, and, finally, indicate some of the factors or conditions that result in productive project management.

What is project management? This question may be answered by examining the definitions which have been presented by persons in this field. Baumgartner (2) defines project management as ". . . the actions involved in producing project deliverable items on time, within the

contemplated cost, with the required reliability of performance. . ."
Cleland (3) defines project management as ". . . the means of managing large aggregation of resources across functional and organizational
lines of authority." Gaddis (6) discusses project management in terms
of the project manager's ability to use the brain power of professionals
and specialists in the creation of a product from its initial conceptual-
ization, through testing, to production. These definitions can be summarized to indicate that the project manager's principal role is the
production of a product by integrating professional persons into a
team. This team which operates within some lines of organizational
responsibility and authority, also operates within time, cost, and performance parameters.

   These definitions, while useful for providing a general orientation,
do not result in a full understanding of the nature of project management or the role of the project manager. We need, therefore, to consider the concept of a project as well as the nature of management,
the organizational placement of projects, and related topics. This chapter will primarily emphasize the nature of project management and
its role in the organization. Subsequent chapters will deal with general
nature of management.

Characteristics of Project

   An understanding of project management requires some familiarity
with the general nature of projects and the characteristics which help
to distinguish these activities from what might be called non-project
activities. Gaddis (6) defines a project as ". . . [an] organizational
unit dedicated to the attainment of a goal—generally the successful
completion of a development product on time within the budget, and
in conformance with performance specifications." Woodgate (22) defines projects as ". . . work to be done or procedures to be followed in
order to accomplish a particular [project] objective." Robertson (18)
defines a project as ". . . the accomplishment of a number of actions
in series and/or parallel in order to reach an objective." An examination of these definitions can help to establish some of the common
elements that exist among them as a means for differentiating project
activities from non-project activities. The following four characteristics
can help us in this differentiation (11).

   First, projects are usually finite in character. There is usually only a
single objective to be accomplished and the project terminates upon
the accomplishment of that objective. Furthermore, the objective

normally is set within some time, cost, and performance specifications. This characteristic does not mean that only a single objective is involved. In many cases multiple objectives may be involved. Here, the main concern is that at some point in time the objective or objectives will be accomplished, and, at that point, the project will be terminated.

Second, projects are usually complex in nature. They usually involve a large number of tasks which must be completed by personnel and other sources in order to accomplish the established objective. Projects can differ in their degree of complexity. Projects of short duration, for example, three months, designed to accomplish a limited objective would not be as complex as projects lasting three or four years and culminating in the achievement of several objectives using many various resources. There is not yet a specific criterion concerning the degree of complexity. There is, however, a large number of individual tasks which have to be completed to accomplish the goal.

Third, a project consists of a series of tasks which relate only to that project. Therefore, it is possible to distinguish the project from its environment and also from other projects which might exist in the same environment. Each project consists of a unique set of tasks which relate only to the individual project. It is possible, therefore, to form a boundary line between the project and the rest of its environment. We can say that a project is unique within itself, unlike other projects in the environment around it. One major problem is the establishment of boundary lines so that only the tasks related to the project can be identified. It is helpful to think of the project as a system and therefore amenable to the concepts, principles, and procedures of systems analysis. We shall return to this consideration in Part II.

Fourth, a project generally consists of a once-through, non-repetitive, or a one-of-a-kind activity. A particular project will be done only once. Any one project will not be repeated even though other projects similar to it may be undertaken. For example, the construction of a particular school building is a non-repetitive project even though other school buildings will be built. The particular school under consideration will not be constructed twice. Research and development projects by their very nature are non-repetitive efforts. One of the major problems in non-repetitive activities, however, is the small amount of historical and objective information which can be used to establish the time, cost, and performance specifications as well as the specific tasks to be done. This type of uncertainty, which pervades many small and large scale research and development projects, is one of the major characteristics of projects. Unfortunately, it also presents a formidable management problem. Consequently, there is a need to develop and utilize techniques in the management of educational development projects that help the project manager to deal with the uncertainty problem.

We can determine whether or not we are dealing with a project or non-project situation by re-casting the characteristics of the situation as a series of questions. If we answer the questions in a positive manner, then we are concerned with a project and the techniques presented in this book are appropriate. Should we be unable to answer the questions in a positive manner, we are probably dealing with a non-project and the techniques presented here probably are inappropriate.

The Placement of Projects in an Organizational Context

A proper understanding of the nature of project management and the function and duties of the project manager requires an understanding of the place projects have in an organizational structure. In this discussion it is assumed that most projects will be housed or placed in an existing educational agency rather than a specially created independent agency. In large projects a specially created agency may exist but these situations are not typical. Usually the project is placed within an existing organization. Four general types of project placement and their relative advantages and limitations will be discussed.

Separate organization approach.   In this approach the project is placed within the organizational structure but remains completely independent of any existing functional units or departments. The project is self-sufficient with regard to the project requirements. All personnel fall under the project manager's authority. Staffing is provided either by transferring personnel from other departments or by hiring personnel from outside sources. This unit is dissolved upon the completion of the project, and the staff members return to their original departments or leave the organization.

The project manager in this approach, has direct control over all of the dimensions of the project. The chief executive of the organization is the main line of authority. One major limitation in this approach is the loss of the project staff assembled for conducting the project upon completion of the project. In this situation if the organization is unable to place these people in other areas, it can lose the services of some valuably trained specialists.

Vertical or Centralized Approach.   A second approach to project placement in the organization is to locate the project in a vertical line

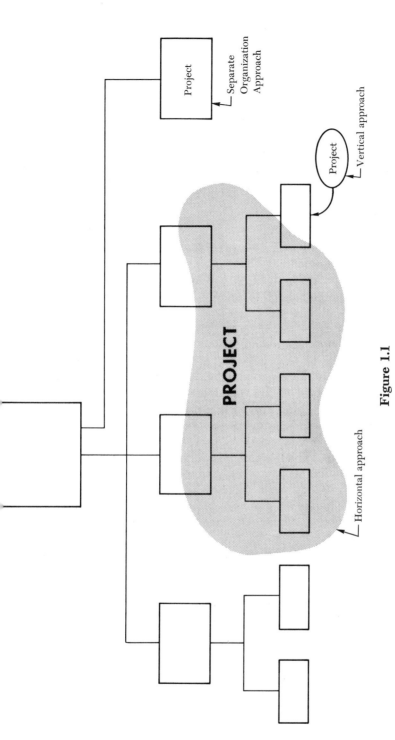

Figure 1.1

Organizational Placement Of Projects.

7

unit, or department. All the necessary project staff are drawn from that department and placed under its administrative head. In this approach, the lines of authority and responsibility are known to all the persons working on the project. The functional department may or may not have the staff to work on the project. If they do not, individuals may be drawn from other functional units and placed in the department for the duration of the project. Individuals may be employed from outside the organization to work on the project. This approach has the advantage of well-known lines of authority and responsibility. However, since these arrangements can lead to new and powerful units as individual projects increase in size and number, it often results in "empire building." If the empire becomes big enough, the organization may find a sub-unit of one department reaching the level of a major department. This approach is infrequently used because of the problems of securing competent staff from within the department as well as the problem of "empire building."

Horizontal or decentralized approach.   The typical approach to project placement involves superimposing it upon the existing vertical and horizontal structure with known lines of responsibility and authority. The project becomes a horizontal unit working across the vertical organizational structure. The personnel needed to work on the project remain within their departments or functional units. Project tasks are assigned to the functional units as they are required. The project manager is responsible for the completion of the work. He generally has authority over the *what* and *why* of the project, while the functional department manager usually retains authority over the *how* of the project. This approach is limited by the project manager's lack of authority over the functional areas in which the project tasks are accomplished. Because of this lack of authority, a large single purpose project which crosses functional organizational lines of authority causes unique management relationships and requires a new management philosophy. The traditional functions of superior-subordinate lines of authority are difficult to apply since the project involves the coordination of many people working under departmental heads whose authority and responsibility lines are vertical rather than horizontal.

The executive staff approach.   In some circumstances, one or more projects may exist in an organization, perhaps in functional units, and one person serves as a staff assistant to the chief executive. The staff assistant's responsibilities are to coordinate, analyze, and make recommendations about project situations, but the final decisions are made by the chief executive. Under this arrangement, the individual placed in direct charge of the project cannot function effectively as an integrator and decision-maker as these roles have been taken out of his hands. This type of approach is similar to the role of the "expeditor" in many organizational units.

Project staff approach. This arrangement usually consists of a project manager who has a staff available to carry out processes such as scheduling, task and cost control, and other special functions unique to the project. The functional departments still perform the majority of work associated with the actual completion of the project. This approach requires considerable coordination between staff and functional departments. It is closely allied to the decentralized approach.

The typical approach is the placement of the project within an existing organization. An individual or a staff is in charge of the project. In these situations, certain general problems arise which make project management difficult. Frequently, functional departments are more interested in their own specialties than in contributing to a unified project effort. Often, the total perspective of the project is lost as actions are taken without regard to their effect on the total project. Decisions pertaining to the project are slow and difficult to make, and information relative to the problems must be obtained from various functional departments through several channels. The nature of projects often requires a rapid adjustment to new situations. In many cases, functional departments are not flexible enough to handle these adjustments. It is the hope of developing solutions for these situations and their problems which has created an interest in project management.

RESPONSIBILITIES OF THE PROJECT MANAGER

With the possible exception of the executive staff approach, the responsibilities of the project manager tend to be the same in the other approaches. The project manager is the focal point for the total project effort. The major project considerations concerning time, cost, and performance are channelled through his office. It is his responsibility to provide a means for integrating and systematizing decisions, policies, and managerial priorities for the various functional and organizational elements. He becomes personally involved in critical project decisions. Since he works with professionals in functional departments as well as with the higher levels of management, he serves as a "go-between" for these two groups. Consequently, he must not only understand the technical research and development problems but also the management problems and concerns.

The project manager develops the project plan. He must recognize that advanced planning is a vital part of effective project management. He must be able to identify the objectives of the project as well as the major events or completion points. His major concern, among other things, is with the amount of detail and realism in the project plan. The project manager must realize that most of the crises or problems which develop in a project usually occur because of the absence of advanced planning.

The project manager controls the project at all times. Schedules, budgets, and performance specifications must be put together in a way that permits him to know what actions to take and when to take them. He must recognize that he is probably the only person in the project who can integrate the *what* and *why* of a particular task with the *when* and *how* of it. The problem of control is acute since he is concerned with the management and conservation of the funds entrusted to him by the funding agency.

The project manager is responsible for developing the project staff. The necessary personnel with the requisite skills must be secured at the proper time and place. The team spirit which exists or does not exist among the members of the project staff may be a consequence of his lack of concern about this responsibility. Through his initiative, the managerial dimensions of the project team will be developed to facilitate the successful completion of the project.

These responsibilities cannot be delegated to other individuals in the project. Certain operational activities, such as the recruitment of personnel, may be delegated to others but the final decision in these activities is his responsibility.

Problem Areas in Project Management

Studies of the project manager's role have identified certain problems. The prospective project manager should be familiar with these problems.

Most research and development projects involve a number of professional persons with specialized skills. The traditional superior-subordinate role becomes inappropriate when working with these individuals. These professionals often are concerned with how the task is accomplished and may conflict with the project manager who is more concerned with the what and when of task accomplishment. The project manager must recognize the implications of asking professionals to produce on schedule and must be aware of the effect of this demand on their professional modes and manners of operation. He must recognize that many professionals like to work toward perfection which may delay the total project effort.

Most projects are finite in their time dimensions. Therefore, the project manager's assignment will terminate unless the project is renewed. Impending project termination may cause a project manager to become more concerned with his future status than his present situation. As a consequence, the final activities associated with the project may be neglected as the project manager devotes his time and energy to preparing new proposals. Because of this situation, educational institutions and agencies must develop some procedures or systems which will assure the project manager that some position continuation will be available upon project completion or until funding for a new project becomes available.

One major problem area has been noted: the typical project manager has few, if any, lines of authority over staff members in other departments. Other techniques or manifestations of authority must be employed in order to accomplish the project tasks. The project manager must draw upon his persuasive abilities, reputation, rapport, influence, status, and prestige to accomplish the project tasks. He must also be able to use the lateral agreements made between the projects and other organizational units. The project manager's basic authority lies within a type of *de facto* authority which comes with the awarding of project funds. His ability to use these funds as a means of authority becomes an important part of project management.

Sometimes, projects are placed in organizations in a way that prevents the project director from having effective control over the schedules, budgets, and performance dimensions of the project. Other functional unit department heads may control the decisions regarding these three dimensions. Specialists in project management generally agree that this is an undesirable arrangement. The inability of the project manager to develop any meaningful relationship between these three dimensions of a project may mean that corrective actions will not be taken at the appropriate times. Placing these three dimensions under the direct control of the project manager assures that there are plans, controls, and an organization for finishing the job. The project director may be given an executive rank within the organization in order to ensure that the parent organization attends to his requests. It may be helpful to offer orientation meetings to the existing organizational structures and units regarding the role of the project manager in order for him to secure their cooperation.

The project manager's undue concern with trivial details of the project is one major problem area. His primary concern should be on operating on an "exception" basis. His time and energy should be devoted to the identification and solution of the critical problems in the project, not the minute details or noncrucial problems. He should realize that the absence of problems may be as indicative of trouble as continuous crises.

If the project manager is only concerned with the management of projects, the long range development of the organization and personnel may be hindered. The priorities assigned to projects may upset the stability of the organization and interfere with the accomplishment of its functional task. Shifting of personnel from project to project may disrupt the training of new employees and specialists and hinder their growth. Possibly, the lessons learned in one project may not be communicated to another project. The project manager, therefore, must be aware of the impact the project will have on the organization. He must not only work to promote the efforts for which he is responsible but also to integrate his efforts with the total organization so that unnecessary conflicts do not arise, and the total organization moves forward.

Factors Leading to Effective Project Management

The successful project may depend frequently more upon the effectiveness of the project manager than upon the technical dimensions of the project. We shall now consider some of the factors or conditions that lead to effective project management.

The project manager should have experience and background in the areas of education which relate to the substance of the project. No one person can be competent in all areas of education, but he should have the fundamental knowledge which can be augmented to deal with the details of a specific operation. His educational background should not only relate directly to the field of education but also to an understanding of management concepts, particularly planning, controlling, and decision-making.

In addition to understanding the preceding management topics, the prospective project manager must be familiar with the general technology of scientific analysis and integration. He should be able to analyze a problem into its component parts and, in turn, integrate them into the total effort. Training in the scientific method, therefore, becomes an important tool in the preparation of project managers.

If it is possible, a person anticipating assuming the role of project manager should have some previous experience as a project manager or director. Lacking direct experience as a project manager, participation in a project as an associate project director will often provide him with the background needed to assume the role of project manager. The experience gained as a research associate will frequently offer the prospective project manager an awareness of the management problems discussed in staff meetings and his need for training.

The role of the project manager is so important that training programs, specifically designed to develop the skills needed in project management, should be established. Several efforts are already under way in this direction. It would seem desirable that the training for project management should be a part of the training for research and development projects in the field of education which might be conducted under the auspices of a funding agency such as the United States Office of Education. This type of knowledge can be obtained in short courses offered by various management associations and agencies. Educational institutions and agencies could develop short term programs which would focus upon the problems and procedures associated with project management. The training would be devoted specifically to the role of the project manager. Furthermore, participation in training courses concerning the general nature of management is also valuable.

Effective project management depends upon organizational support and resources. The lack of support can be a disrupting factor in the success of the project manager and his project. If he does not have the time and assistance he needs to carry out the many duties associated with the project, or if he finds himself involved in conflicting lines of authority, the whole project can be jeopardized. Obviously, if the project manager is given the responsibility for the total project, the organization should give him the support he needs to ensure the success of the project.

References

1. Andrew, Gwen, "Some Observations on Management Problems in Applied Social Research," *The American Sociologist*, II, No. 2 (May 1967), pp. 84-89.
2. Baumgartner, John S., *Project Management*. Homewood, Ill.: Richard D. Irwin, Inc., 1963.
3. Cleland, David I., "Why Project Management?" *Business Horizons*, Vol. VII (1964), pp. 81-88.
4. Davis, K., *A Preliminary Study of Management Patterns of Research Project Directors in Manufacturing in the Phoenix Area*. Tempe, Arizona: Western Management Science Center, Arizona State University, 1961.
5. Dearden, John, and F. Warren McFarlan, *Management Information Systems: Texts and Cases*. Homewood, Ill.: Richard D. Irwin, Inc., 1966, Chapter 4.
6. Gaddis, Paul O., "The Project Manager," *Harvard Business Review*, XXXVII No. 3 (June 1959), pp. 89-97.
7. _____, "The Project Manager . . . his role in Advanced Technology Industry," *Westinghouse Engineer*, XIX, No. 4 (July 1959), pp. 102-06.
8. Gibson, R. E. "A Systems Approach to Research Management," in *Research, Development, and Technological Innovation*, James R. Bright, ed., Homewood, Ill.: Richard D. Irwin, Inc., 1964.
9. Groueff, S., *Manhattan Project: The Untold Story of the Making of the Atomic Bomb*. New York: Bantam Books, Inc., 1967.

10. *Guidelines for Improving Project Management*, Proceedings of a workshop for Title III, ESEA Directors, Division of Research, Planning, and Development, Ohio Department of Education, 1969.

11. IBM Systems 360, *Project Management System 360 Application Description*. H20-0201-0, White Plains, New York: International Business Machines, 1966.

12. Keats, E. S. "How to Become a Good Project Manager," *Aerospace Management*, (August 1963), pp. 20-23.

13. Krugman, H. E., and H. A. Edgerton, "Profile of a Scientist Manager," *Personnel*, XXXVI, No. 3 (Sept.-Oct. 1959), pp. 38-49.

14. Mahan, A. V. *Criteria for the Use of Project Management*, Unpublished Master's thesis, Graduate School of Business Administration, Ohio State University, 1966.

15. Mahoney, T. A. "Predictors of Managerial Effectiveness," in *Building the Executive Team*, Englewood Cliffs, N.J.: Prentice-Hall, Inc., 1961, pp. 186-97.

16. Middleton, C. J., "How to Set up a Project Organization," *Harvard Business Review*. XIV, No. 2 (March-April 1967), pp. 73-82.

17. Mooney, Ross, "Problems in Initiating a Project," *Theory Into Practice*, Vol. V (June 1966), pp. 139-43.

18. Peck, M. J., and R. M. Scherer, *The Weapons Acquisition Process: An Economic Analysis*. Graduate School of Business, Harvard University, 1962.

19. Robertson, D. C., *Project Planning and Control*. Cleveland, Ohio: Chemical Rubber Company, 1967.

20. Steiner, G. A., and W. G. Ryan, *Industrial Project Management*. New York: The MacMillan Company, 1968.

21. Stewart, J. M., "Making Project Management Work," *Business Horizons*, VIII, No. 3 (Fall, 1965), pp. 54-68.

22. *The Views of 920 PACE Project Directors*, Report No. 5 of the Second National Study of PACE, Office of Education, Washington, D.C., November 20, 1968.

23. Woodgate, H. S., *Planning by Network*. London, England: Business Publications, Ltd., 1964.

chapter 2

The Nature and Functions of Management

Management, as a concept, has been defined, formalized, and taught for less than sixty years. Yet, management has existed since the establishment of the first organization, whatever it might have been. This statement is not the result of an empirical study but, rather, an inference drawn from the fact that man is a social animal who has always tended to join with others in organizations of some sort and for some purpose. This purpose, whether expressed or implied, was accomplished through methods based on hit-or-miss, past experience, and the use of available thought processes, and not through a specific checklist of functions.

Taylor, Fayol, and Barnard produced pioneers writings on management just after the start of the 1900's. The study of management has been dominated largely by persons connected with business enterprise. As a result, there has been the tendency to equate management with business and to dismiss generalizing to other disciplines. Management is, however, applicable to a variety of disciplines and its general functions are useful in each discipline. Only the techniques of applying the various functions change from discipline to discipline and situation to situation.

Simply stated, management is getting things done through

people. If the definition is expanded, it is the attainment of organizational goals by creating an environment which is favorable to the performance of the people belonging to the organization. The essential implication of the definition is that management involves people and not material. Although a certain amount of raw material put into a machine may never vary, a certain amount of input to an individual will not yield as predictable an output as the machine. Several factors, social, psychological and intellectual, combine to affect this output. In essence, it is the manager's job to keep these outputs as predictable as possible.

Functions of Management

A manager accomplishes his task by performing certain management functions. However, few authors agree on the several functions per formed by a manager. The classical management functions which will be described in this section are: *planning, organizing* (including staffing), *directing* (including motivating) and *controlling*. Figure 2.1 illustrates the four functions and shows the relationships that exist between them.

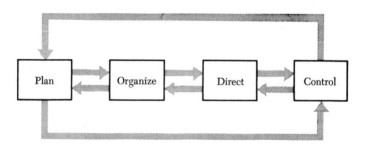

Figure 2.1

Functions Of Management.

Before discussing each of these functions, however, a distinction should be made between the terms *management* and *administration*. Various authors use the word administration as a synonym for management. Indeed, many high level positions in the field of education carry the title of administrator. We consider these positions to be basically managerial positions since the four functions are carried out by persons holding these offices. Management, here, is considered a process involving a high degree of uncertainty and unprogrammed decision-making. Administration, here, is considered a process involving a high degree of certainty, highly structured actions and programmed decision-making. This definition of administration follows the concept of the management function discussed by Simon (11).

The manager determines policy; the administrator executes it. This statement might be exemplified through a comparison of the actions of a dean or executive committee of a college which determines entrance requirements, and the actions of an individual who admits students based on their fulfillment of the specified criteria. This, of course, is an over simplification of actual processes but does serve as an example.

The manager gathers the diverse elements of information to aid him in making a decision for which there are few procedural guidelines, but the administrator has his actions controlled by a standard operating procedure or a checklist. When a situation requiring a decision arises, the administrator consults his checklist to determine his course of action.

Positions within an organization are not exclusively managerial or administrative. Individual positions have characteristics or requirements which are examples of both situations. In this respect, management and administration are the end points of a continuum into which most job positions fall. As a general rule, administration becomes more dominant at the lower organizational levels, and management becomes more dominant at the higher levels. This suggests two possible problem areas. First, it is human nature for an individual to avoid uncertainty and concentrate on the situations which are familiar and routine. This can lead to difficulties if it is done at the expense of managerial requirements. Second, there is a tendency for the individual to apply a programmed decision process to situations which are unique and unprogrammed. This may result in the failure to account for, or evaluate fully, all the variables in the situation and therefore reach an incorrect conclusion.

Both the field of education and the field of business use the concept and functions of management as they are outlined in this chapter. Education, in contrast to business, uses the term *administrator* in place of the term, *manager*. The position taken here is that the role of the manager differs greatly from that of the administrator.

Planning

If any one managerial function could be labeled as the primary function, it would be planning. The basic step in planning is the establishment of objectives, goals, and purposes or functions. Objectives are so fundamental that a few more basic and important points should be made. First of all, the primacy of objectives is inviolate. They are the end of all action. They channel planning and guide organizing, directing, and controlling. They are the most important consideration in decision-making, no matter in which area of management it occurs. Second, objectives are not the same between organizations. They vary with the type of organization and the circumstances involved. Third, objectives must be practical. They should be set at a point in time which can be reached. Fourth, objectives should be broken into long range and short range objectives, and the accomplishment of short range objectives should support the accomplishment of long range objectives. Finally, a hierarchy of objectives usually can be established for either an organization or a project. It is difficult for an individual to work effectively or efficiently without definite goals. Unless these goals are specified by the organization, an individual may have to specify his own goals even though they may be the wrong ones, or may not contribute to organizational or project objectives.

Planning is the definition and evaluation of alternative courses of action, and the selection of one alternative course which can be used most effectively and efficiently to satisfy the requirement of a balance between long and short range goals. Planning as a process results in a set of initial decisions which are considered necessary to accomplish the future state of affairs desired by the planner (1).

The formulation of plans takes several forms which are usually inherent to all formal organizations. An *objective* or *goal* is one type of plan and is prerequisite to planning. Objectives are the end of a plan. *Policies* are a second type of plan. They are generally statements or understandings which guide or channel thinking in decision-making. Policies can be either written or unwritten, but more consistent results are obtained if they are written, thus leaving less room for individual interpretation. Policies can be derived by either formal declaration or as a result of certain types of action in specific circumstances. It is difficult to declare policies that will cover all situations, and, if declared, they can have additional negative effects by stifling individual initiative. A third type of plan is a *procedure*. Procedures emphasize a chronological sequence and are guides to action. The procedures belonging primarily to administrative positions are the practices which are so recurrent and routine that they lend themselves to formalized responses. *Rules* are similar to procedures as they state a course of action. Rules differ from procedures as they are required courses of action which allow for no deviation, while procedures serve as guides to action. Usually procedures do not specify time, while rules relate action to a time frame. The *budget* is also a type of plan since it is an attempt to relate cost to a plan of action. Most educational planners are primarily concerned with the *program* or *project* plan. The program is a complex of policies, procedures, rules, tasks, and associated elements which are necessary to carry out a given course of action and achieve a stated objective. A final type of plan which is more frequently found in business management than in education is *strategy*. Strategy is a plan made in light of changes or expected changes in the external environment.

The importance of planning is self-evident, but there are certain points which deserve mention. As Le Breton and Henning (9) have stated, any plan deals with the future and should indicate the action to be taken by people. A plan that does not involve the three elements of future, action, and people is not a complete plan. Simply because a plan focuses upon the future, there are problems. As the future is unknown, we are always dealing with a degree of uncertainty when we develop a plan. Planning can offset this uncertainty by organizing a specific course of action and developing contingencies for the unexpected. Since the end in planning is the attainment of objectives, planning serves to focus attention on them. By planning for the efficient use of time and materials, a more economical operation can be gained. Finally, planning is the prerequisite of control. It is difficult to imagine an effective control system that does not have a specific process to control.

The statement that planning is a key function in the management process is not valuable if an individual does not know how to plan. Certain steps or procedures are valuable in the planning process. Planning begins with the establishment of objectives. A desired end must exist before a plan can be formulated. The second step is premising. Premises are informed estimates of future conditions. Whereas a plan relates to action which will occur in the future, or to the final result of an action, premises attempt to predict what these conditions will be. The third step is the definition of alternatives. Several courses of action usually exist for any objective. Defining only one course of action neglects the possibility that there might be a better course. Developing alternatives leads the planner to evaluate his alternatives. After more than one course of action has been defined, the planner must decide which course of action is better. This will require applying a decision-making process to the stated alternatives in order to decide which one will be more effective in accomplishing the objective.

The evaluation of alternatives is one of the most difficult and important steps in the planning process. One possible method available for this step is the *means-ends analysis*. Means-ends analysis is a logical break down of the methods or alternatives available to attain a desired end, or objective. Analysis begins at the objective or the "end" and proceeds through the various means for reaching it until one of the following happens: (1) a means is found unworthy of further consideration because it is not feasible or another means is better; (2) a point within the alternative (a sub-end or sub-goal) cannot be reached as there are not adequate means to attain it; or (3) a means is reached which is known to be feasible.

Once the plan has been chosen, the planner is ready to begin implementing it. This is accomplished, either by creating an organizational unit (a project team), to carry out the plan, or by implementing it through the existing organizational structures. At this point the planner has reached the management function of organizing.

Organizing

Organizing establishes an integrated system of activities and authority relationships through which the project members can learn what their tasks are, their position in the overall scheme and possess the requisite authority to accomplish these tasks. Organization has evolved because of what is known as the "span of management control", which simply means that there is a limit to the number of individuals a manager can effectively supervise. This number is dependent on several variables, some of which are the intelligence of the manager, the competence of his subordinates, and the type of activities performed. When the maximum number is reached by a manager, he has reached his optimum span of management. Organization then becomes an attempt to realize optimum spans of management, grouping activities and individuals. The principal advantage of organization is efficiency, and, once again, the overriding consideration in designing an organizational structure is the accomplishment of the objectives.

The two terms most frequently associated with organization are authority and responsibility. Authority, as it is used here, is the right to command others or to take or not take action. The definition of responsibility is based on authority since it is the obligation to use authority in order to have the work performed correctly. Authority becomes the binding force of organization. Some confusion exists about the distribution of authority and responsibility throughout an organization. It is often said that responsibility is delegated to subordinates. A consideration of the definitions of authority and responsibility, however, indicates that this is not true. Authority to command or act is *delegated* to subordinates and responsibility is *exacted* from subordinates. Obviously, the proper delegation of authority is not valuable unless the responsibility of the subordinate to use it is exacted from him.

Related to the concepts of authority and responsibility is the principle of *unity of command.* Simply stated, unity of command means that a person should not have more than one superior. If an individual receives orders from two different people, confusion, frustration, and ineffectiveness will probably result. It is difficult enough to satisfy one superior, let alone two.

The principle of unity of command is only one of several principles that can be stated from a framework of organization. The *scalar principle* is another principle concerning authority. It states that in any organization, the ultimate authority must rest somewhere and there must be an unbroken line from this point to every sub-level position in the organization. There is also the *principle of delegation* which stresses that, after certain performance levels or results are specified, sufficient authority for their accomplishment must be delegated to the responsible subordinate. The *principle of absolute responsibility* works both up and down the chain of command. In other words, the responsibility of a subordinate to a superior for the authority delegated to him is absolute, but the superior is also absolutely responsible for the activity of his subordinate. Next is the *principle of balance* between authority and responsibility. The exacted responsibility must not be greater than the amount of authority delegated, nor should it be less than the amount of authority delegated. Finally, there is the *principle of the authority level* which states that decisions should be made at the lowest level in the organization in which requisite authority exists and should be referred upward only when this authority does not exist at a lower level.

In an organizational structure that results in departmentalized activity, there are three fundamental concepts which apply to departmentation. The first concept is *division of work.* The activities of the organization should be divided and grouped in a way which will contribute effectively to the objectives. This does not mean simply grouping by occupational specialization. Instead, it is similar to a "subsystem" approach in which each department consist of a grouping of tasks which will most effectively contribute to the organizational objectives. The second concept is *functional definition* which requires that each position and department have a clear definition of the expected activity, delegated authority, and relationships with other positions and departments. The third concept of *separation* emphasizes that an activity which is designed as a check or control on another activity should be assigned to a separate department. This should avoid any bias in the evaluation of the activity controlled.

These concepts and principles, while basic, deal primarily with authority and activity grouping and not the overall organizational process. Three more general principles can be applied to this process. There is first the *principle of balance* which states that the application of these principles and concepts must be balanced and tailored to the organization. Second, the *principle of flexibility,* derived from the dynamic nature of the organization in the modern environment, requires that the application of principles and concepts be sufficiently flexible to permit changes in application due to changes in the organization and its environment. Finally, there is the *principle of leadership facilitation* which deals with the requirement for building into the organizational structure a situation in which the manager can most effectively lead his subordinates.

A sub-function of organization, which is often treated separately, is *staffing.* Staffing is the recruitment, selection, and employment of personnel who are qualified to help attain the organizational objectives. This definition emphasizes an extremely important point about staffing: the organizational objectives must be determined first, and the organization staffed to effectively and efficiently attain them. Objectives must not be tailored to the available staff as this can result in a serious compromise of objectives. This situation would be a negation of the primacy of objectives. There may be situations in which it becomes obvious that competent personnel cannot be obtained to accomplish objectives, consequently, the objectives may have to be altered. There is a fine distinction between this situation and the one just mentioned. We will discuss more about staffing for projects in a later chapter except for one other important principle, the *principle of job definition.* In order to properly and adequately staff an organization, each position must first be given definite specifications that relate to the organization's objectives. This facilitates recruiting as it narrows the alternatives and helps to ensure the "right man" for each position.

Direction

The function of direction is primarily as a process of motivating subordinates. Direction is simply getting employees to accomplish their tasks.

Directions begins the day an employee begins work. Obviously, the orientation he receives is important. Before the new employee can begin work, he must know how his position fits into the departmental and organizational structures, the relationship of his job to other activities, and exactly what is expected of him. In effect, this is simply the continuation of the job definition process begun in staffing.

The orientation process should not end once these requirements have been met. Communication between the manager and his subordinates must continue in order to keep them informed of organizational activities, objectives, policies, and personnel. Once again the method used for this communication can be tailored to fit the situation. The manager may use written communication, memoranda, bulletins, reports, duty assignments, or oral communication, staff meetings, conferences, committees, and individual contact. This communication requirement is frequently overlooked by managers because of its repetitive nature and because managers sometimes become so enamoured with their own routine and problems that they become isolated from those with whom they work. The problems and procedures of communication have led to the development of a specialized function of management which is referred to as *communication theory*.

The motivation of subordinates can be a difficult process, and effective methods will probably differ among individuals. This is particularly true in educational research and development, since a large number of intelligent, competent professionals are usually employed to carry out the project tasks. Each individual has certain basic needs which provide internal motivation. Individual needs can be grouped into categories beginning with the simplest and progressing to the more complex and difficult. These categories fall into the areas of physiology, safety, society, self-esteem and self-fulfillment. The motivation for satisfying at least the basic needs come from sources outside the organization, primarily the family and community. The manager must attempt to determine the level of his subordinates' motivation by increasing or withholding the satisfaction of these needs, and, therefore, achieving the desired level of work.

In addition, the manager must be sure that the personal needs which his subordinates are working to satisfy are in harmony with the organizational interests. Having ascertained this, he must encourage the fulfillment of the needs which will satisfy both individual requirements and organizational requirements.

Control

Ackoff (1) has defined control to be a process of evaluating the initial decisions established in the plan and revising, altering, and modifying the decisions as needed in order to accomplish the plan. Control may be broadly defined as the reaching of planned objectives, or the arranging of events to conform with previous plans. Both definitions contain the same key word, *plan*. Control cannot exist without a plan or until a standard has been determined against which performance can be compared. Yet, before performance can be compared to a standard, the manager must obtain a knowledge of performance. The essence of control is information in the hands of the manager.

A distinction should be made between control and supervision. Supervision is a directive process, a guiding of subordinates in the accomplishment of their tasks. Control involves both the realization that this supervision may not accomplish the desired results and the revision and action upon this situation. Control, like management, concerns people and not material. When deviations from the original plans are discovered, there will be a person who is responsible for the area of deviation. Output may be controlled by controlling the performance of the individual responsible for the output.

The establishment of standards for control can be a difficult process and requires considerable thought. The standards must be set at a level which is attainable with the available resources. Improperly set standards may result in inaccurate reports to the management, stating that a project is behind or ahead of schedule when, in fact, the opposite may be true.

Furthermore, accurate standards tend to take the "human element" out of control. Controlling is centered around people but the reporting of objective results is an attempt to eliminate personality and individual judgment in order to avoid camouflaging either good or substandard performances.

Managerial effort can be wasted however if it attempts to follow every detail of planning execution. While good planning results in a hierarchal structure of plans and sub-plans, the manager should determine where in this plan his responsibility is located and then determine which elements or strategic points of the plan will have the greatest effect on the success or failure of his part of the plan. The breakdown of the plan into a system of sub-plans will usually indicate several strategic points, but the manager should then examine each sub-plan to find the strategic point within it.

The determination of strategic points leads to the principle of control advocated by most authors, the *principle of management by exception*. The exception principle is directly related to strategic points but is not synonymous with them. Strategic point control only concerns recognizing the points to be watched, while the exception principle concerns watching for significant *deviations* between *what is* and *what was* planned at these points. Significant deviations may occur, however, at points other than those designated as strategic. Although points that are not designated as strategic should permit more tolerance for deviation, deviations at these points also can cause the failure of the plan. The control system must be designed to accommodate this factor. Control by exception increases managerial efficiency by permitting the manager to deal primarily with major problems and not the day-to-day details of the project plan.

The design of control procedures which would apply these principles is not a final objective. Adequate controls are of no value unless reported deviations result in corrective action and replanning. Managers must receive not only useable information but also the authority to make decisions involving the information and then, implement their decisions.

There should be a periodic review of any established control system to ensure that it remains an effective tool. Organizational dynamics and future uncertainty lead to changes which may cause the control system to become outmoded. A periodic review will help to keep it applicable to the current operative situation.

The concepts presented here are neither new, revolutionary nor complete. Managerial skill is extremely difficult to learn in a classroom. It is best learned through experience gained in job situations. The concepts taught in the classroom are meant to serve as aids and guides to organizing the manager's operating methods. The following chapter will present a brief outline of how the manager operates on the job or carries into practice the functions of planning, organizing, directing, and controlling. The two functions of planning and controlling will receive the primary emphasis in the remaining part of this text.

References

1. Ackoff, Russell, *A Concept of Corporate Planning*. New York: Interscience Publishers, Inc., 1970.
2. Anthony, Robert N., *Planning and Control Systems: A Framework for Analysis*. Division of Research, Graduate School of Business Administration, Cambridge, Mass.: Harvard University, 1965.
3. Emery, J. C., *Organizational Planning and Control Systems*. New York: The MacMillan Company, 1969.
4. Goetz, B. E., *Management Planning and Control*. New York: McGraw-Hill Book Company, 1949.
5. Johnson, R. A., F. E. Kast, and J. E. Rosenzwieg, *The Theory and Management of Systems*. New York: McGraw-Hill Book Company, 1963.
6. Kepner, Charles H., and Benjamin B. Tregoe, *The Rational Manager*. New York: McGraw-Hill Book Company, 1965.
7. Koontz, Harold, and Cyril O'Donnell, Ed., *Management, A Book of Readings*. New York: McGraw-Hill Book Company, 1964.
8. _____, *Principles of Management*. New York: McGraw-Hill Book Company, 1964.
9. Le Breton, P. P., and D. A. Henning, *Planning Theory*. Englewood Cliffs, N.J.: Prentice-Hall Inc., 1961.
10. Newman, William H., and Charles E. Summer, Jr., *The Process of Management*. Englewood Cliffs, N.J.: Prentice-Hall, Inc., 1961.

11. Simon, H. A., *The New Science of Management Decision.* New York: Harper & Row, Publishers, 1960.

12. Smiddy, Harold F., and Lionel Naum, "Evolution of a Science of Managing in America," *Management Science*, Vol. I, (October, 1954), pp. 1-24.

chapter 3

The Management Process or Cycle

The previous chapter outlined and described several major functions that are carried out by a person designated as the manager. Besides identifying the general functions carried out by managers, individuals who have studied management have derived a series of procedural steps by which a manager operates in a given situation. This series of procedural steps is titled the *management cycle* or *process*. This chapter will describe the general steps in this process, which can be identified as (1) establishing objectives, (2) developing plans, (3) setting up schedules, (4) measuring progress, (5) deciding and acting, and (6) replanning or recycling. Figure 3.1 presents a graphical portrayal of this process. The reader should refer to this figure as he proceeds through the description of each step in the process.

STEPS IN THE MANAGEMENT PROCESS

Establishing Objectives

Every organization, formal or informal, by its nature will have objectives. It is essential, especially to formal organizations in education, that these objectives are firmly established, clearly defined, attainable, and communicated

31

throughout the organization. While the objectives may change, they must not be vague, indefineable, or uncommunicable. The first step in the managerial process, then, is to establish objectives. Objectives

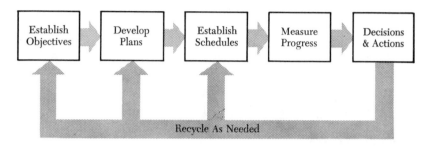

Figure 3.1

The Management Cycle Or Process.

have the effect of providing a framework in which all subsequent management actions will take place. Objectives channel the planning and are a prerequisite of effective planning. The decision-making process will not operate effectively if it is not oriented toward the accomplishment of these objectives.

There are several types and levels of objectives which can be identified. Long range objectives are statements of the organization's intents over an extended period of time. In a means–end situation, they are the ends. If long range objectives are the ends, then short range objectives become the means or the way in which long range objectives can be met. It follows, therefore, that short range objectives must support long range objectives. Obviously there must be a hierarchy of objectives. Once organizational objectives have been established they can be broken into more operable segments and assigned to sub-units of the organization. The breakdown process can be carried to the lowest sub-division of the organization, the individual. The breakdown of objectives gives each sub-unit or individual a definite goal to work toward and facilitates the control process by providing a framework for progress analysis. In a hierarchy of objectives, major or larger objectives are determined first. These are followed by the delineation of necessary sub-objectives which must be accomplished to achieve the larger objective. There is a constant review process to ensure the proper integration between major and minor objectives. This constant review process further ensures that the minor objectives do support the major objectives.

Objectives themselves can take many forms and are often referred to under different titles. Objectives can take the form of producing a report, making a decision, securing data, or acquiring equipment and facilities. Obviously, the more specific we are about the nature of the objectives, the more likely we are to determine if they have been accomplished. This is essentially the reason behind much of the current emphasis on behavioral objectives in the field of education. Objectives also may be referred to as goals, purposes, or functions. Regardless of the term, the step of establishing objectives is concerned with the basic question of *what* we are trying to achieve and *why* we are trying to achieve it. Until we can answer these questions in a meaningful and useful way, it is difficult to carry out the remaining steps in the management process.

Developing Plans

Objectives provide the framework for planning, and planning is a process by which alternative, future courses of action, which will lead to the accomplishment of objectives, are defined, evaluated, and selected. To be a complete plan, any proposed course of action should be oriented toward the future, should indicate the actions to be taken, and should identify who will take them.

As there is a hierarchy of objectives, so there will be a hierarchy of corresponding plans. Planning must pervade all levels of the organization and will become increasingly more detailed at the lower management levels. Rensis Likert (7), a leading proponent of participative management, suggests that the progress of the organization will increase greatly as more individuals from all levels of the organization become involved in the planning and decision-making process. Obviously, an individual will become more involved and interested in a program which he has helped to develop.

Planning involves development and choice of alternative ways of reaching a particular goal. It is concerned with the means for reaching a given end. The major problem is the selection from the other possible plans the means or a sequence of actions which has a reasonable chance of accomplishing the end. Some of the plans that are developed and presented for consideration can be eliminated because they do not satisfy certain dimensions of the objectives. For example, if an individual were asked to give a speech in New York City and had to be there by nine o'clock in the morning and the sponsoring agency would pay only travel expenses from his home to New York City, many alternatives would be available to him. He could travel by bus, train, plane, or even drive. If he drove, he could go many alternative roads. If, however, he stated that his time away from the office should be the least time possible (a modification of the objective) then some of the alternatives would be automatically dropped—bus, train, and private car. In planning, it is important to generate alternatives, so that all possibilities will have been considered before the decision is made.

One of the major difficulties in planning is the uncertainty of the future. We cannot, as we consider alternative courses of action, know what events in the environment will hamper or interfere with the achievement of our goal. It is important, therefore, in developing plans to consider what can go wrong and to develop ways of handling or even preventing the problem in the event that it should occur. We should try to reduce uncertainty as much as possible even though we cannot completely eliminate it. An element or degree of risk will always be present.

Establishing Schedules

Once a plan of action has been adopted, we must establish a time table for the specific actions. This process of placing the plan on a calendar is called scheduling. Many planning and control systems emphasize the establishment of a plan without reference to a schedule. In these situations, a schedule is developed after the completion of the plan. This does not mean that a calendar is not applicable to plan development. As a plan is divided into its constituent parts, time estimates (job duration estimates) are made for each part but the start and completion dates for these parts are not set. This procedure, it is thought, avoids biasing time estimates in favor of calendar dates. Once schedules have been established and implemented, they become an extension of the plan and serve as controls.

Several factors influence the scheduling step, and the availability of resources is probably the single most important factor. Resources in this context include personnel, both their quantity and quality (technical ability), money, facilities (including make or buy situations) and time. Time becomes increasingly important when plans have an *assigned* completion date. It is important to maintain an independence between time estimates and scheduled (assigned) completion dates. Time estimates should be made first and completion dates assigned to them. If the estimated time will result in a time overrun, then a revision of the plan must occur. Other factors influencing scheduling are the desire for the efficient utilization of personnel and facilities, and the evaluation of time estimates by other personnel to account for tendencies to either "pad" time estimates or to overestimate personnel abilities.

Measuring Progress

Once a plan goes into operation, management needs to constantly check the progress or performance. In general, this process is referred to as control which is discussed in a specific chapter later in this book. For our immediate purposes, control of the accomplishment of the plan is achieved through communication devices generally referred to as *progress reports*. Although a plan seldom remains unchanged throughout the life of its implementation, it does provide the manager with a set of standards by which he can determine if the planned actions are going properly. The essence of control is noting a deviation from these planned standards, determining why the deviation has occurred, and taking corrective action. The greater the precision in planning, the greater the potential for effective measurement of progress and control.

One major problem in measuring progress is that of providing management with the proper information regarding present progress. The manager must be provided with this information quickly and in such a form that any significant deviations are readily identifiable. At this point, the principle of management by exception becomes important. The deviations reported to management can be both positive and negative. In some cases, progress will be better than was expected, while in other cases, progress will not be as well as expected. In either case, management needs to know these situations so that the proper adjustments can be made.

The general process of measuring and reporting progress is commonly called "feedback." If reports to management are going to be useful, the feedback must be rapidly accomplished and contain accurate and useful information. Here the major problem is the separation of "noise" from "signal." The more we can eliminate noise or irrelevant information from the progress reports, the more likely it is that management can deal effectively with the problems presented.

Decisions and Actions

It is unlikely that a project will be completed exactly as it was planned. Progress reports will indicate where and how much any deviation has occurred. The preparation and presentation of progress reports is pointless unless management plans to act upon the situations presented in the report. If a deviation that shows an operation behind schedule is presented, management must do something about it. Some replanning efforts must occur in order to remedy the situation presented. This requires management to decide upon a corrective course of action. As in the initial planning situation, the manager must consider alternative solutions before making a final decision. He must decide if a proposed course of action will indeed remedy the situation.

Recycling

After a consideration of the problem and its possible solutions, a decision must be made which will correct the problem. Actions are then taken to readjust the plans or to correct any deviations. This recycling process may include not only adjustments in the schedule but also may involve a reexamination and adjustment of the original objectives and the plan developed to accomplish them. In general, any management actions taken to correct deviations should avoid changing the original plans. In some cases, however, extensive revision may be necessary. Recycling or readjusting the plan is a necessary managerial step. In many situations, problems are identified but no corrective action is taken which causes the original situation to become a more serious problem at a later time.

The steps we have outlined can be summarized under two general steps: *planning* and *controlling*. In this case, planning would include the process of establishing objectives, developing plans, and establishing schedules. Controlling would include the process of measuring progress, then deciding and acting, and recycling as needed. The planning steps establish what *should* happen in a project while the controlling steps indicate what is *actually* happening. The managerial process is basically one of establishing the *shoulds* and then making sure that *actual* performance is consistent with them. If it is not, then necessary adjustments should be made to establish conformity with the original plan, or the total operation should be adjusted to a new or modified set of standards.

THE MANAGER'S ROLE IN THE MANAGEMENT PROCESS

To gain a more complete understanding of this process by which management operates in a given situation, we need to consider the specific role that the individual project manager plays in the total process. The primary role of the manager is decision-making. Simon, in his book the *New Science of Management Decision* (12), equates management with decision-making. He then goes on to state two general categories of decisions which might face a manager: programmed and non-programmed decisions.

Programmed decisions are usually repetitive and routine. If and when a problem occurs, a routine set of rules and regulations for the situation is available. The availability of these rules and standard operating procedures leads to a more certain decision and offers uniformity of action over a period of time.

Non-programmed decisions are those which are unstructured, novel, and seldom occurring. Routine procedures for these situations have not been developed either because the problem has not occurred before, or because its structure cannot be confined within defined parameters, or because it is so important that it deserves individually designed treatment. In these situations, the decision-maker must rely upon his general capacities and his own problem-solving techniques.

Not all the decisions faced by a manager fall into the programmed and non-programmed categories. It is perhaps best to imagine a continuum with the two types of decisions as end points and the degrees of each type in between them.

Regardless of the type of decision involved, studies of the decision-making process itself have demonstrated that the process is effective only to the extent that information is available to the decision-maker. The manager must make decisions relevant to the selection of goals, development of plans, and assessment of progress. Figure 3.2 illustrates

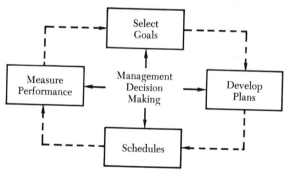

Figure 3.2

The Manager As A Decision-Maker.

this major role of decision-maker. Because of the importance of information in decision-making, numerous systems have been developed over the past several years to provide managers with the information needed for effective decision-making.

A management information system provides timely, accurate, and valid data to management. This does not mean that the system is easily designed to fit all steps in the managerial process. Information requirements vary with the type and source of the management function. The designer of a management information system must consider this when attempting to construct a formal system.

Both the importance of information and the differentiation of information according to need are stressed in Anthony's excellent discussion of planning and control systems (2). He identifies three levels of management: strategic planning, management control, and operational control. These three levels form the pyramid, shown in Figure 3.3. Strategic planning concerns the general process of deciding upon the objectives of an enterprise, the changes in objectives, and the general policies that govern the acquisition, use, and disposition of

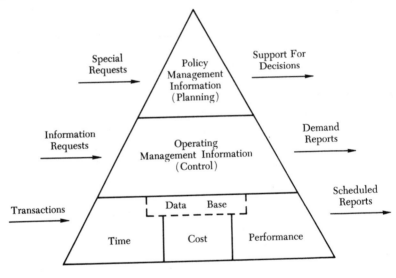

Figure 3.3

Project Management Information System. (After Robert Head. Reprinted with permission from © Datamation, May, published and copyrighted 1967 by F. D. Thompson Publications, Inc., 35 Mason St., Greenwich, Conn.)

resources. Management control concerns the processes which insure that the resources are obtained and used effectively and efficiently. Underlying each of these levels is the need for the appropriate information. While it is only a generalized model for planning and control systems, the model is relevant to the development of information systems within the project management situation. Figuratively, the project director is concerned with strategic management, his assistants are concerned with management control, and the persons working on the staff are concerned with operational control.

The development of a project information system is similar to the general development of a planning and control system. It follows the same general breakdown according to the levels described by Anthony. The daily transactions occurring within a project result in numerous pieces or elements of information. These form what is called a *data base*, shown in Figure 3.3. This data base is somewhat unstructured and unorganized for management use, but the organization and structuring of these elements of information into meaningful and related groups will result in detailed reports which can be used by managers at both the operational and management control levels. Further organization, structuring, and separation of the data elements will result in information which will be useful to the strategic planning level and to the top levels of management control. The data base within either a project or organization is valuable to all levels of management. An information system design must concentrate on organizing and structuring the data in a way which will be useful to each level. The design must also concentrate on processing the data through periodic reports or upon special request, so that it can be available on a regular basis.

Irrespective of any function for which a system is providing information, certain general objectives and principles of design must be remembered. Moravec has outlined some of the objectives that should guide the development of a management information systems (9). It should provide each level of management with the fundamental information that can be used in each manager's job. It should filter information so that each level and position of management receives only the information that it can and should act upon. It should provide information to the manager only when action is possible and appropriate. It should be capable of providing the analysis, data, or information in any form that is requested. It should always provide information that is up-to-date. Finally, it should provide information that managers can understand.

The design of an information system presents several problems which must be considered. The data base containing the unorganized elements of information must be organized and structured, but at the higher levels of management the need for detail decreases while the need for summary and trend display increases. If the needs of each management level cannot be met by restructuring and distilling the data base, then each level will require its own data base from which to acquire information. Another difficulty arises when the functional units use the same data base. Each unit has different requirements and a tendency to design its own data base, which frequently results in the duplication of effort and information. This situation poses a serious challenge to the system designer who must develop a system which can serve all functional units. A manager may require details of past experience or current interests in his area. The problem is not to design a system which is appropriate for this manager but to design a system which will not require a major revamping with the advent of a new manager. Finally, there is the matter of cost. Before designing or installing a system, there must be a consideration of the costs of the system and its benefits. It is possible that increasing the volume and rapidity of information through an information system is not the crucial part of the system. Perhaps, by increasing the accuracy and validity of an existing manual system, increased benefits can be obtained at a fraction of cost.

Information Needs of Project Managers

Until now, we have discussed the general nature and objectives of management information systems. We still do not know the specific information needs of persons responsible for planning and controlling projects. Numerous studies of this problem have identified three general categories of information that are needed: time, cost, and performance information.

Time information relates to total project time, individual tasks times, schedule dates, and directed completion dates. It is important that, at all times, the project manager knows exactly how far the project has advanced in terms of the initial schedule established in the planning phase.

Cost information primarily concerns the expenditure of funds or the utilization of resources, including personnel, materials, and services. The project budget is a plan which shows how expenditures will be made during the life of the project. It is important for the project manager to know how the money is spent. The project manager must have in his possession information relating to the rapidity of expenditures as well as slowness of expenditures.

Performance information concerns the question of quality control relative to the objectives initially set forth, product specifications, accomplishments of personnel on a task, and related items.

While each of these types of information can be discussed independently, it is important to realize that, in a project situation, the three types of information represent variables which interact with each other. Their interaction is shown in Figure 3.4. If each type of information is considered as a variable which is independent of the other types of information, changes in one can affect the other. For example, if there is a schedule slippage, it may be that the only way to recover it, is through the expenditure of more funds, or increased costs. If performance specifications are not met within established time and cost dimensions, then these dimensions may have to be changed in order to meet the performance specifications. The interaction is such that if one variable is held constant, manipulations can be made only on the other two. It is possible to conceive of an optimum relationship between all three that would enable the project to be completed on time, within cost, and performed satisfactorily. Adjustments always would be necessary to develop this optimum arrangement, but they could not be made, however, without an information system that would provide the project manager with a comparison between planned time, cost, and performance and the actual conditions at any given time. The three types of information that make up the data base for a project are shown in Figure 3.4.

Only a total integrated management system, would provide the three types of information in a form that would allow the interactions to be carefully appraised. Present management information systems are not that far advanced. While there are information systems generated for each of the three major variables, usually the information is not interrelated.

In the next chapter we discuss some of the information systems that have been developed over the past several decades. Each of these systems has its advantages and limitations. None of them does a complete job by itself. Regardless of their respective qualities, the major function of these systems is the establishment of a data base relative to time, cost, and/or performance. In general, the primary elements are established in the planning phase of the project and are used subsequently to carry out the control phase.

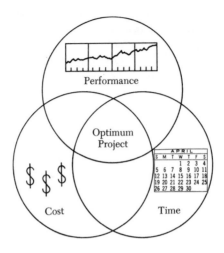

Figure 3.4

Interrelationship Between Time, Cost, And Performance.

SUMMARY

This chapter has outlined the general steps of the management process which include establishing objectives, developing plans, estab lishing schedules, measuring progress, deciding and acting and recycling as needed. The manager must make decisions for each of the steps in the process. Decisions cannot be made, however, without information. The types of information needed by a project manager relate to time, cost, and performance. Several systems have been designed to provide one or more kinds of information. The next chapter will discuss some of these systems as they are used in the project management situation.

References

1. Andrew, Gary M., and Roland E. Moir, *Information-Decision Systems in Education.* Itasca, Ill.: F. E. Peacock Publishers, Inc., 1970.
2. Anthony, Robert N., *Planning and Control Systems: A Framework for Analysis.* Division of Research, Graduate School of Business Administration, Cambridge, Mass.: Harvard University, 1965.
3. de Hanika, F. P., *New Thinking in Management.* London, England: Hutchinson and Co., Ltd., 1965.
4. Doyle, Lauren B., "Perpetual User Studies," *Datamation,* XII, No. 10 (October, 1966), pp. 28-30.
5. Head, Robert V., "Management Information Systems: A Critical Appraisal," *Datamation,* XIII, No. 5 (May, 1967), pp. 22-27.
6. Koontz, Harold, and O'Donnell, Cyril, ed., *Management, A Book of Readings.* New York: McGraw-Hill Book Company, 1964.
7. Likert, Rensis, *New Patterns of Management.* New York: McGraw-Hill Book Company, 1961.
8. Meadow, Charles T., *The Analysis of Information Systems.* New York: John T. Wiley & Sons, Inc., 1967.
9. Moravec, Adolph F., "Using Simulation to Design a Management Information System," *Management Services,* III, No. 3 (May-June 1966), 50-58.
10. Newman, William H., and Charles E. Summer, Jr., *The Process of Management.* Englewood Cliffs, N.J.: Prentice-Hall, 1961.
11. *PERT . . . Guide for Management Use.* PERT Coordinating Group, Office of the Secretary of Defense, Washington, D.C., 1963.

12. Simon, Herbert A., *The New Science of Management Decision*. New York: Harper & Row, Publishers, 1960.
13. Woodgate, H. S., *Planning By Network*. London, England: Business Publications Limited, 1964.

chapter 4

Project Management Systems

The previous chapter outlined the general procedure by which a manager operates in a given situation. To assist the manager in these operations, numerous techniques have been devised. These techniques can be characterized as *management systems*. This chapter will discuss some of the management systems which have been developed for use in project situations. In order to understand these systems, the reader must have some idea of the general concepts and principles underlying them.

Introduction to Systems Concepts

The current approach to the analysis of many disciplines is called the *system approach*. Scholars in all fields have realized the universality of certain ideas, such as classification, grouping of events, and the breakdown of processes and phenomena which have led to a greater understanding of the discipline. Because of this universality, the development of concepts in a particular discipline has resulted in a greater understanding of the discipline.

45

A system is defined as a logical arrangement of interdependent and interrelated parts which become a connected whole in order to accomplish a specific objective. *System analysis* is the process of reducing the system into its interdependent parts. The process of reassembling these parts into an integrated whole is referred to as *system synthesis*. The principal value of a system approach is its ability to account for the factors affecting the achievement of the objective. The tasks of analysis and synthesis are not easy because a requirement of systems design is the inclusion of all factors which affect it.

To define a system as a collection of interrelated and interdependent parts designed to accomplish an objective still does not fully describe the nature of any system. To be a complete system, several elements must be included in it. Nadler has outlined seven basic elements which make up any system (11).

1. Each system must have a *function* which is the aim, purpose, or mission of the system.
2. Each system must have *inputs* which can consist of information materials, and energy.
3. Each system must have *output* which is the end result of converting the inputs.
4. Each system must have *sequence* which is the process of steps which converts the inputs into outputs.
5. Each system exists in an *environment* which can be physical and/or attitudinal in nature.
6. Each system must have *equipment* and *human agents* which aid in converting the input into output but do not become part of the output.
7. Each system must have an *information feedback loop* to permit adjustment of inputs, sequence, and output as needed to accomplish system function.

Each of these seven elements will exist to some degree in any system. Sometimes, one element may become confused with another element. For example, the *output* of a system is often confused with the *function* of the system.

In addition to the seven elements necessary to make up a system, there are two additional characteristics which are important. Usually systems are *hierarchical* in nature. That is, larger systems are made up of smaller systems. Second, systems can be categorized as *deterministic* or *probabilistic*. Deterministic systems are those systems in which the interaction of components or elements can be predicted without the risk of error if the facts or information which the system must handle are known. Probabilistic systems are those systems in which the functioning of the system is at a level that prohibits strong predictions of outputs according to given inputs. In the following sections, we will use both the hierarchical and the deterministic-probabilistic characteristics to discuss the various management systems that have been developed.

Project Management Systems

Working from these basic concepts and characteristics, a *project management system* would be a system which would have as its function the task of providing the project director with a way to manage a project. It would emphasize particularly the planning and controlling functions of management. This system would have the basic system components outlined by Nadler. For example, the documents which would outline tasks to be done and schedules to be maintained would be outputs from the scheduling and task outlining phases which, in turn, would have their inputs and process steps. These types of outputs would enable the project manager to carry out his task more efficiently. Numerous systems have been developed over the years to aid the project manager in his work. Obviously, the number and variety of these systems prohibits their full discussion in this chapter. The systems we will discuss represent generic types rather than specific descriptions.

It was noted earlier that systems could be characterized as deterministic or probabilistic. If a given project has well established goals and procedures, then the situation is deterministic. If, however, the goals, the sequence of tasks to accomplish them, and the associated time and costs are uncertain, then the situation is probabilistic. For example, the construction of a school building would be deterministic, while a project concerned with a new or revised curriculum might be probabilistic. The project management systems described below have been developed for each of these situations. Before deciding which management system is appropriate for a given situation, the project manager must decide on the basic nature of the project. Unless some thought is given to this problem, the project manager may select the wrong techniques and find it difficult to manage the project.

The development of project management systems dates back to the early part of this century. Their development began with the introduction of the Gantt Chart by Henry L. Gantt. We will trace the development of the Gantt Chart, Milestone Chart, precedence diagramming, and network diagramming (PERT/CPM). Each of these techniques utilizes the systems approach to a project situation, although the terminology of the systems approach did not gain prominence until World War II.

These techniques can be divided into two classes according to the breakdown of general systems. Gantt Charts and Milestone Charts are concerned primarily with production functions and, therefore, are closely related to deterministic systems. Precedence and network diagramming were developed for project situations possessing large degrees of inherent uncertainty and, therefore, are more probabilistic.

The use of the first two techniques, Gantt Charts and Milestone Charts, in project planning is limited since their major value lies in their application to repetitive functions. Yet, they are valuable to certain aspects of a project management situation. The use of precedence and network diagramming techniques is more beneficial because these techniques are more closely related to a general system and can be easily adapted to meet the problem at hand.

The Gantt Chart. In 1917, Henry L. Gantt was hired as a consultant to the United States Munitions Factory at the Frankford Arsenal. Gantt had done research on production techniques and efficiency and had realized that the essential element for scheduling production was time, not quantity. Prior to his work, time was used only in a past tense form. That is, to record events as they occurred but never as a planning medium. Gantt applied his realization to his already developed techniques of graphical control with satisfactory results. Upon the declaration of World War I, Gantt's techniques were expanded to the entire Ordnance Department.

Gantt developed three basic charts. His first chart was the Progress Chart, which is a general planning and control chart. It is a horizontal bar chart plotting each working period against scheduled tasks as shown in Figure 4.1. Scheduled start and completion dates are indicated by brackets positioned along the time scale. Progress is represented as a percentage of the time between the brackets. If the progress bar does not extend to the point which represents the current date, then the task is behind schedule. Correspondingly, if it touches or is beyond this point, the task is on schedule or ahead of schedule. His second charts were the Man and Machine Layout Charts. These are two separate charts which have the same general purpose of illustrating the effective utilization of men and machine by plotting the actual performance or nonperformance and the use or lack of use of each against a time scale. These are planning charts used for scheduling work rather than controlling it. Finally, there are the Layout and

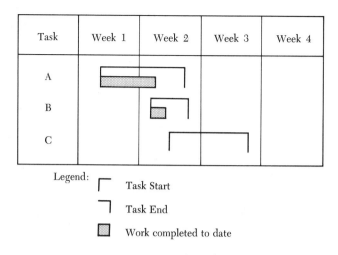

Figure 4.1

Basic Schemata Of Gantt Chart.

Load Charts. Gantt realized that scheduling operations often requires the sequencing of machine to machine, man to man, man to machine, or machine to man. While some idle time is inevitable, the Layout Chart was planned to make the best possible use of available men and machines. It also facilitated replanning as it presented a comprehensive step by step layout of a function. Load Charts are similar to Layout Charts since they also show the work to be done. However, they differ from Layout Charts in that the work is shown by class of machine or men, and not by single operations. They further differ from Progress Charts in that they show only the future, not the past.

There are several advantages to the use of Gantt Charts. In the first place, they make planning necessary. Second, they compare what was planned to what was accomplished. By bringing out the time relationship, they emphasize why the performance has fallen short of the expected performance. Furthermore, they present facts so that future events can be foreseen. They are compact, and they point out gaps in information. Finally, they are easy to draw and read, and aid in visualizing the passage of time, thus helping to reduce waste and idleness.

There are, however, certain limitations to the Gantt Charts. They do not adequately recognize the interdependencies existing between the efforts represented by bars. The static scale makes it difficult to reflect the dynamic nature of plans and their susceptability to change. In addition, the charts are unable to reflect uncertainty or tolerance in their estimation of time. Furthermore, they are best applied when the process is repetitive and well defined, rather than when the process is new and untried.

Milestone Charts. Milestone Charts were developed after the Gantt Charts. They established control points within a plan and are used primarily for progress reporting and control. When they were first developed, Milestone Charts were a further refinement of the Gantt Charts which did not indicate any critical points or specific sub-objectives. Milestone Charts identified certain sub-objectives and facilitated control by measuring progress in terms of milestone completion. An illustrative Milestone Chart is shown in Figure 4.2.

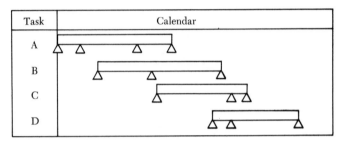

Figure 4.2

Illustration Of Simple Milestone Chart.

Milestone Charts are not a complete system within themselves. They are a technique which can be applied or added to other systems to increase their effectiveness. Currently they are being used with network systems primarily for reports and for associating costs with the completion dates. The milestone system applies cost by groups of activities rather than by individual activity. It then statistically derives the activity cost rather than requiring the operating level personnel to keep this type of detailed information.

The Milestone Charts facilitated definite progress reporting and the development of sub-objectives, thus giving operating personnel something to work toward as well as the completion of the overall objective. However, it was only an improved technique to be used with existing systems. It did not show any greater interrelationship of activities than did the system to which it was applied. Furthermore, it did not easily or adequately differentiate between critical and noncritical areas. It has little use as a predictive tool.

Network Systems. Within the past ten years, a different approach has been taken and new techniques of planning and controlling have proven highly beneficial to managers of nonrecurring, or one-time only projects. These techniques can be classified under the heading of Network Analysis System and more aptly classified as precedence diagramming and Program Evaluation and Review Technique/Critical Path Method (PERT/CPM). These new techniques represented a major advance in management capabilities. Methods were developed which resulted in the complex breakdown of a project into its component parts (system analysis) and then its reorganization into a network of tasks (system synthesis) which depicted the complex interrelationships and dependencies of the tasks upon each other. Figure 4.3 provides an illustration of both approaches.

The major difference between Precedence Diagramming and PERT is the representation of work tasks, or as they are called by both systems, *activities.* In Precedence Diagramming, activities are represented by circles and are connected by dependency arrows; in PERT, activities are represented by arrows and the circles to which they connect (called events) represent instantaneous points in time, those instances where an activity is started or completed. When PERT is used, it often requires dummy activities or arrows representing no time to illustrate the dependency of one task on another. Precedence diagramming eliminates this need by containing all time passages within a circle. To some practitioners, this represents an advantage by eliminating dummy activities. It does result in a simplification of the network by eliminating events. Consequently, its concept is sometimes more readily grasped by operating personnel. These advantages, however, may be disadvantages to other operating personnel. Precedence diagramming eliminates events which, in some instances, may be important, as, for example, in Milestone Reporting. Furthermore, the use of events allows for the integration of various sub-networks through interface events. This is not possible with a precedence diagram. Tracing a path through the network is more difficult with precedence diagramming since the linkage between event numbers which PERT employs is not present.

CPM was introduced in 1957 by Dupont and Sperry-Rand while PERT made its appearance in 1958 in connection with the development of the Navy Fleet Ballistic Missile System. PERT was developed by the Navy Special Projects Office, Lockheed Missiles and Space Company, and the consulting firm of Booz, Allen and Hamilton. Early applications of CPM were primarily to construction and engineering projects, while PERT was applied mainly to government

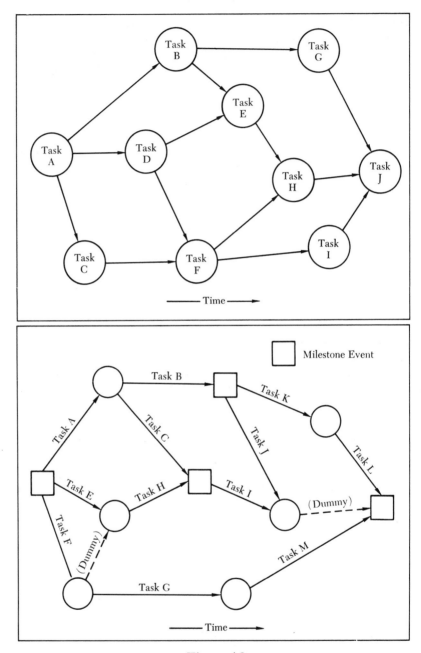

Figure 4.3

Illustration Of Precedence Diagram And PERT/CPM Network.

research and development projects. They are similar in their application to new, unique, and one-time only projects.

Their advantages are numerous and cover the major limitations listed for previous systems. First, they force and result in better planning, scheduling and control. They depict the comprehensive interrelationships of tasks to the total project and yield a better assessment of current status of a project. They aid proposal preparation and aid replanning through simulation methods. Furthermore, the uncertainty of time estimates can be statistically analyzed. Finally they facilitate the "management by exception" principle.

This book will emphasize the network-based management systems. This choice is based on the assumption that the typical educational research and development project is best planned and controlled by using this technique because of the uncertainty that exists within these projects. This does not mean that the other techniques have little or no value for educaional projects. They have been and are being applied in many practical situations. The remaining chapters of this book will be devoted to describing how management systems are developed for a given project situation.

While each of the previously described systems has its advantages and limitations as well as its areas of application, it would be more useful to the potential project manager to grasp the underlying principles of these systems so that he can develop his own system for management of a project situation.

References

1. Archibald, Russell D., and Richard L. Villoria, *Network-Based Management Systems (PERT/CPM)*. New York: John Wiley & Sons, Inc., 1967.
2. Boulding, Kenneth E., "General Systems Theory—The Skeleton of a Science," *Management Science*, Vol. II (April 1956), pp. 197-208.
3. Clark, Wallace, *The Gantt Chart*. New York: The Ronald Press Co., 1923.
4. Cook, Desmond L., *A New Approach To the Planning and Management of Educational Research*. Columbus, Ohio: Educational Program Management Center, Ohio State University, October, 1964.
5. Cook, Desmond L., *Better Project Planning Through the Use of System Analysis and Management Techniques*. Columbus, Ohio: Educational Program Management Center, Ohio State University, November 1967.
6. Handy, H. W., and K. M. Hussain, *Network Analysis for Education Management*. Englewood Cliffs, N.J.: Prentice-Hall, Inc., 1969.
7. de Hanika, F. P., *New Thinking in Management*. London, England: Hutchinson & Company, Ltd., 1965.
8. Goldfarb, Nathan, and William K. Kaiser, *Gantt Charts and Statistical Quality Control*. Hempstead, New York: Hofstra University Yearbook of Business, 1964.
9. Department of the Navy, Office of Naval Material, *Line of Balance Technology*. Navexos P1851 (Rev. 4-62).

10. Miller, Robert W., *Schedule, Cost, and Profit Control with PERT.* New York: McGraw-Hill Book Company, 1963.

11. Nadler, Gerald, "Engineering Research and Design in Socio-Economic Systems," in *Engineering*, A. Riesman, ed., Madison, Wisconsin: University of Wisconsin, 1967.

12. Starr, Martin Kenneth, *Production Management Systems and Synthesis.* Englewood Cliffs, N.J.: Prentice-Hall Inc., 1964.

13. Wattel, Harold L., ed., *The Dissemination of New Business Techniques: Network Scheduling and Control Systems (CPM/PERT).* Hofstra University Yearbook of Business, Vol. II (January, 1964).

14. J. H. Greene, *Operations Planning and Control.* Homewood, Ill.: R. D. Irwin Inc., 1967.

part 2

Project Planning and
Controlling Procedures

The previous section provided an orientation to the unique but emerging role of the project manager in the field of education. Proper understanding of his role requires background concepts in management functions, processes, and systems.

The discussion of the functions presented in Chapter 2 stressed that the end product of the planning process was a set of initial decisions called a plan. The concept of the control function was discussed as a case of evaluating these initial decisions and then revising them as needed in order to achieve the original objectives of the project. Major questions focus upon what decisions does the project manager have to make, how does he make them, and how does he revise them? This section will discuss these questions.

To clarify what decisions have to be made and how they are made, the section has been divided into chapters which focus upon decision-making in the time, cost, and performance dimensions of the project. Chapters 5 and 6 present the procedures involved in making initial decisions about performance. Chapter 7 reviews how decisions are made about the total project time and individual work task time. Chapter 8 reviews the procedures involved in scheduling the project and allocating resources. Chapter 9 illustrates the many kinds of cost decisions that have to be made. The concept of control as a decision review and revision procedure is presented in Chapter 10.

The section concludes with a chapter that presents a generalized project management model under the acronym PACT, or Planning and Controlling Technique. An understanding of the material presented in the chapters preceding the model is needed in order to properly implement the model in practice. The objective of the model is to enable the project manager, acting or potential, to have a means of developing a planning and controlling system which fits his unique situation.

chapter 5

Project Definition

The basic step in applying planning concepts to educational projects is project definition. The success or lack of it in carefully defining the nature of the project under consideration is a fundamental factor to the overall success of the project. Woodgate (14) has illustrated the importance of the project definition step as shown in Figure 5.1. He has shown it as the base of the pyramid which represents the total planning function.

The project manager must understand the purpose of this step since it can help him to achieve the subsequent steps in the total planning process. Before discussing the nature and process of project definition, some general considerations about this step should be discussed.

Project personnel at all levels of the project, management and operations, should be involved in the project definition phase. The involvement of prospective project personnel in this operation can increase the possibility of securing from them commitments to carry out the work of the project. Many people working on a project often can contribute ideas about the nature of the tasks that cannot be developed by a single person. Not all project staff need to participate at the same time. However, they should be involved at some

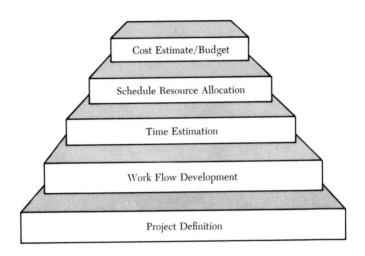

Figure 5.1

Planning Systems Pyramid. (After H. S. Woodgate.)

time during the process of project definition. Usually, the group involved should be not much larger than three to five people since larger groups tend to operate ineffectively in this process. A relatively small planning group can take their work to the remaining staff members for discussion and possible revision.

An inadequate initial project definition may result in unnecessary problems during the course of the project because it has failed to consider all the relevant tasks. The omission of a significant work effort because of a failure to spend the necessary time on the initial outline of the project may result in the need for revision as the work progresses. Therefore, it is essential for the planning group to allow themselves enough time to carry out this activity thoroughly. The time spent in developing the project definition can save time in the later stages of the project activity.

Different people can devise different definitions or analyses for a given project. Not all people will identify the same set of activities for a given project. Each person on the staff will have his idea of how the project should be carried out. Under these circumstances, there must be an effort to secure a statement of the project tasks that is acceptable to all the individuals concerned in the project. In the event that different people identify a similar set of tasks within the project, it is possible that a standard model has been or can be developed. This situation is likely to develop when the project is one in which the planning group has had prior experience. For example, a project involving the development of a test may be more quickly defined since the process of developing a test is well established and described in many discussions of test construction. Conversely, difficulty in reaching a project definition may reveal the project to be unique. It is possible that there are no previous models or experiences that can be used to establish the project definition. This problem may arise in a research situation even though some standard tasks have been developed.

UTILIZING THE SYSTEMS APPROACH IN PROJECT DEFINITION

The process of project definition advances on the assumption that a project is best viewed as a system and that the principle of the hierarchical nature of systems is then applicable. For readers who are not familiar with the nature of systems, we can define a system as a combination of interconnected and/or interrelated tasks needed to accomplish an objective or goal. Figure 5.2 presents a general illustration of a system broken into component parts represented by levels.

It is assumed that any given research or development project can be conceived as a system since it also consists of a series of interrelated and interdependent tasks that must be accomplished in order to reach the major objective of the project and its necessary sub-objectives. It

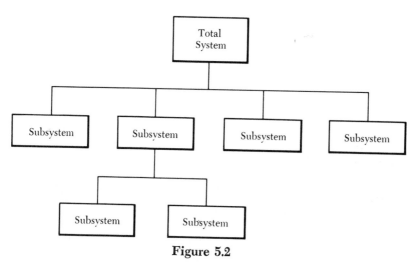

Figure 5.2

Illustration Of A System.

is further assumed that the objectives of a project are also hierarchical in nature, i.e., for each project there are usually several sub-objectives which are needed to accomplish the larger objective. We might, therefore, speak of the major or prime objective, second level objectives, or third level objectives. Establishing the hierarchical nature of these objectives is an essential process step in the development of the project definition.

A system is said to exist within an environment as represented in Figure 5.3. The environment affects the system which, in turn, affects

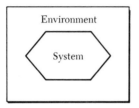
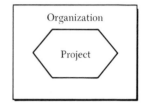

Figure 5.3

Systems And Projects In Their Environments.

the environment. The environment usually provides certain limits and constraints within which the system must operate. A project also exists in an environment which is usually an organizational structure, and is affected by it. The environment of the project also provides limits and constraints, usually in the form of schedules and budgets but sometimes in the form of specified accomplishments which have a decided impact upon the project. The major task is a definition of the project which will allow the elements composing it to be separated from the environment in which it exists. This is essentially a process of establishing boundary lines for the project. The process of project definition includes an attempt to determine not only what should be included in the project but also what should not be included in the project. The criterion for the inclusion of a task as a project element is the answer to the following question: Does this job, or task relate to the accomplishment of the overall project objective?

Viewing the project as a system permits us to use the principles of disassembly and assembly provided in system analysis. Collectively, these principles are a useful vehicle for the project definition activity shown in Figure 5.4. The principle of disassembly means that we subdivide the project into its component parts, subsystems, units, and similar segments. This is an analytical function. Once we have identified the component parts we can then employ the principle of

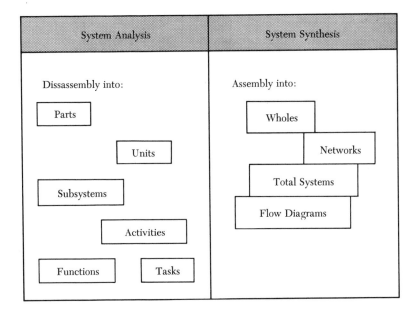

Figure 5.4

Nature Of System Analysis And Synthesis.

assembly and establish wholes, total systems, networks, and other presentations of totals. This is a process of synthesis or integration. Within the planning system, the process of project definition employs the principle of disassembly. The construction of the work flow, which is discussed in the next chapter, is an employment of the process of the assembly principle, or, as it is sometimes called, "system synthesis." The process of project definition is essentially the application of the system approach to a project situation. It is impossible, within the confines of this book, to discuss all aspects of the systems approach. The reader may consult several of the references appearing at the end of the chapter if he is interested in securing more information on the application of systems approaches to problems.

The systems approach described in this chapter should not be new to the reader. It is similar to the process of outlining which is commonly used in the preparation of speeches and term papers. For example, a speech normally has three parts: an introduction, body, and conclusion. While each of these parts bears some relation to the other parts when thinking about the total speech, each component can be considered by itself. Each component has an objective associated with it. The work of preparing the introduction results in that section of the speech being completed. This one objective, however, should not be confused with the objective of the speech itself, which may be informing people, or motivating them to action. This objective will be considered in the work involved in producing the introduction. Using a systems approach, we can outline the preparation of a speech like the outline in Figure 5.5. We could take the

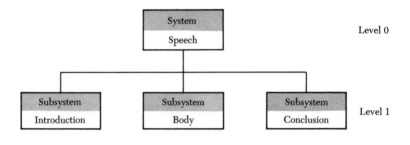

Figure 5.5

A Speech Using A Systems Approach.

introduction section and break it into at least two additional parts, a humorous story plus a statement of speech purpose. If we did, these would be smaller subsystems making up the subsystem labeled introduction at Level 1. A similar analysis of the other subsystems would identify similar parts which would need to be accomplished in order to produce the related subsystems.

Process Steps in Developing the Project Definition

The product of the project definition phase is referred to as the *workbreakdown structure* (WBS). The workbreakdown structure defines the project tasks, or work to be performed, and establishes a relationship between the tasks and the major project objectives. The workbreakdown structure also establishes the framework for the scheduling and control of the project. It functions to establish a framework for summarizing the schedule and cost status of the project at progressively higher levels of management. It is not unusual for the workbreakdown structure, once completed, to correspond to the levels of the organizational structure in which the project is based. This does not, however, always happen.

The planning of any activity begins with the definition of objectives or goals to be reached by the activity. Since most projects are complex, objectives must be defined or established for each subdivision or sub-unit of the project. Project definition, therefore, is a process which involves the development of an explicit statement of the project's primary objective and the necessary sub-objectives to reach the major goal. It is important to recognize that the objectives or goals of a project can take several forms and can include the development of hardware items such as physical equipment, softwear items such as reports and working documents, decisions, and the development of processes. The reader will probably note that work or task accomplishment is strongly emphasized. The accomplishment of each objective is usually expressed in terms of the product which represents the accomplishment of that objective. We do not state the objective explicitly but, instead, indicate what will be the result of achieving it. For example, an objective which is focused upon the development of a textbook is expressed as "textbook." In this description, it is understood that the work involved will lead to the accomplishment of the objective, the development of the textbook. This approach enables us to focus on units and sub-units more quickly than we could if we became involved in trying to describe *functions* or *processes* rather than products. It is easier to specify when the work is accomplished if we are able to describe the characteristics of the product rather than the characteristics of the process or function involved in producing it. Hence, the employment of the term workbreakdown structure.

The normal procedure in project definition or the establishment of the workbreakdown structure is a general to specific procedure which ensures that the entire project will be fully and properly related to the total project objective. It also ensures the total integration of the project in terms of the hierarchical ordering of tasks that will accomplish the objective and the integration of the objectives themselves on a hierarchical basis. This procedure also helps to assure useful summaries of project information for management reports.

The first step in project definition is a mission statement which contains the major goal of the project and a recognition of limits and constraints important to the project. For example, a mission statement for a recent training program conducted at the American Educational Research Association meetings was:

> . . . to design, develop, produce, implement, and evaluate a five day educational research management training program for an AERA presession within the limits and constraints established by AERA.

This major goal or project mission statement was translated into the final end product. In this case, the end product was "AERA Presession Program." The product is placed at the top level in Figure 5.6. The total effort is then subdivided into further sub-objectives which represent the major work units needed to accomplish the overall objective. These subsystems or objectives are further divided into more detailed statement of work. The process of subdivision continues to successively lower levels. At each level, the complexity of the work is reduced until the smallest unit of work is determined for planning and control. The smallest system, objective, or work effort is commonly referred to as a *work package*. A work package is a specific job, often within the responsibility of an operating unit in an organization, which contributes to one item on the workbreakdown structure. Each work package is a clearly defined, specific implement of accomplishment. A work package may represent a design, a document, a piece of equipment, or a service. In contrast to the total time and cost for the project, work packages are usually relatively short in duration and low in costs. Each work package should have a definite start and end point in terms of the process steps involved in producing the item.

One major problem in developing the workbreakdown structure or project definition is the amount of detail which should be shown. What should be the minimum size of the work package? How many levels should be developed? A specific answer to these questions is not possible since there is no present research to indicate what might be possible criteria. There is, however, an answer to this question from the management point of view.

The size of the work package or the number of levels shown or the amount of detail exhibited in a workbreakdown structure depends upon how much detail the manager wants to plan and control during the operational stage. If too much detail is shown, or the work packages are too small in terms of the time and costs involved, too much control might exist. In other words, a great deal of time and energy will be devoted to planning and controlling relatively small items. If not enough details are shown, or not enough larger tasks are broken into smaller ones the manager may lose control as he has no way of keeping an adequate account of work progress. There must be a balance between the size of the work packages, the amount of detail, or the number of levels, and certain factors which relate to adequate planning and control. Some of these factors will include the degree of complexity for the total project, the extent to which various work packages will be assigned to organizational units, the past performance of individuals or organizational units in accomplishing a particular

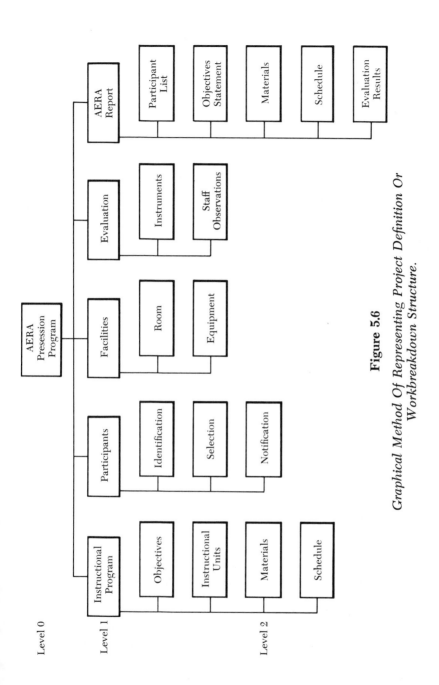

Figure 5.6

Graphical Method Of Representing Project Definition Or Workbreakdown Structure.

67

piece of work, and the cost involved. Should a relatively large work package be developed, then some of these factors will not be visible. Yet, too much detail regarding some of the factors may result in a work package that is relatively small and unnecessarily detailed.

For some cases, the military has formulated a set of criteria for the development of the workbreakdown structure. For example, they might suggest that a workbreakdown structure be broken down to a level in which the smallest work package is a job that takes six months and costs less than $100,000. Applying these criteria to a large scale project involving millions of dollars is reasonable. We do not presently have sufficient experience in the field of education to know how these same criteria of time and cost can be used to set limits for work packages or the amount of detail in a project.

The project definition or workbreakdown structure can be represented by either a graphical procedure or a tabular outline. Figures 5.6 and 5.7 which exhibit the project definition for the AERA training program illustrate these two approaches.

Before discussing the two methods of workbreakdown structure representation, we should discuss the general nature of the project. The basic purpose of the AERA program was a five-day instructional session on research management procedures. This program was to be conducted during the week before the regular American Educational Research Association convention. This particular project has been selected for illustration because of its relative simplicity in discussing the process of project definition. Examples of more complex projects, larger in time and scope of work, are presented later in this chapter.

The tabular method of representing a project definition, or workbreakdown structure is presented in Figure 5.7. This illustration shows the five major sub-objectives needed to accomplish the total program objective. Each of the objectives has been expressed as an end item to be produced as a result of the accomplishment of the objectives at lower levels in the representation. In developing the workbreakdown structure for project definition, it is useful to focus upon a statement of end products (instructional programs) rather than upon the functional steps (develop instructional program) since the end products are the exact nature of the output to be produced as a result of the work accomplished at lower levels. In this example, the five major end items were the instructional program, the participants, the facilities, the evaluation, and the final report for the American Educational Research Association. Each of these five sub-objectives or end items was broken into smaller objectives. For example, under the instructional program a list of instructional objectives was to be produced, the

Tabular Method Of Representing Project Definition Or Workbreakdown Structure.

0	1	2	3	4
AERA Presession Program	Instructional Program	Obectives	General / Specific	
		Instructional Units	Introduction and Orientation to Management	Research Management / Nature and Process of Management / Management Systems
			Program and Project Management	Project Management / Project Selection
			Project Planning	Project Definition (WBS-Systems Anal.) / Project Planning (Networking) / Project Scheduling (Resource alloc., time est.) / Budget Preparation, costing, "PERT/cost"
			Project Control	Management Reports / Prob. Anal. and Decision Making / Recycling
			Multiple Project Management (Program)	PPBS / "RAMPS" (CEIR)
			Organization and Implementation	
			Summary and Review	
		Materials (Resources)	Explanatory Monograph / Exercise (games, simulation, etc.)	

0	1	2	3	4
		Daily Schedule		
	Participants	Identified (by AERA)	Publicity Application Materials	
		Selection	Criteria Number	
		Notification	Draft Letter Mailing Advance Materials	
	Facilities	Room	Reservation Arrangement	
		Equipment	AV Other	
	Evaluation	Instruments	Daily Reaction forms Total Reaction forms AERA Developed Staff Developed	
		Staff Observations	Director Other Staff	
	Report for AERA	Participants	Names Attend. Records—# only	
		Statement of Objectives		
		Listing + 2 copies of Materials	Instructional Evaluation	
		Evaluation Results	Instrument Summaries Critique Results Director Written Observations	

instructional units established, the necessary supporting instructional materials developed and prepared, and the daily schedule established. Each of these sub-objectives is expressed as a product output. For example, the schedule was thought of in terms of a piece of paper which would show the sequence of topics and exercises according to days of the week and the hours of presentation. This objective would be accomplished when the piece of paper which would show the actual schedule, had been developed. Each of the other four major end items are also broken down at level 2.

One disadvantage to the graphical method becomes apparent when the project is complex. It becomes difficult to show additional levels in detail since the actual working document is large. As a result, it is not possible to show easily in Figure 5.6 the additional details which would support the accomplishment of each of these sub-objectives at level 2. For this reason, we have an expressed preference for the tabular method of representation which is shown in Figure 5.7.

The tabular method of representation follows exactly the level concept shown in the graphical method in Figure 5.6. In this illustration, level 0 is shown at the extreme left, followed by level 1 in the second column. The work which will accomplish the objectives at level 1 is shown in level 2 and corresponds to level 2 of the graphical method in Figure 5.6. The illustration in Figure 5.7 shows additional detail at level 3 and 4. For example, the sub-objective of instructional objectives at level 2 has been further divided at level 3 into general and specific instructional objectives. The objective of the instructional unit has been broken into 7 additional objectives at level 3 with each of these objectives broken into further detail at level 4. Inspection of the Figure 5.7 reveals that some items were broken into further detail at level 4 and some were not. The new details were added at levels 3 or 4 only when it was desirable to show additional work which had to be accomplished at those levels and for which planning and control had to be exercised. At each of the additional levels of breakdown, there are at least two subunits of work that have to be accomplished. As a general rule, if there are not at least two or more items of accomplishment at the succeeding lower level of detail, the development of the workbreakdown structure should be terminated at the next higher level. It should also be noted that no time sequence is reflected in the workbreakdown structure. The sequencing of activities in their order of accomplishment on a time dimension is represented by the project plan which was developed. If any sequence is represented by the workbreakdown structure, it can be thought of in terms of reading from the bottom up on the graphical method and from the right to left on the tabular method. For example, the objectives at level 4 represent work which has to be accomplished to reach the objective at level 3. The accomplishment of work at level 3 represents the accomplishment of objectives at level 2 while the accomplishment of objectives at level 2 leads to the accomplishment of objectives at level 1. When all of the level 1 objectives have been reached the entire Presession Program will have been defined.

A workbreakdown structure for a larger project designed to study the applicability of network techniques to the field of educational research and development is shown in Figure 5.8. This project covered a total time of 18 months with a budget of approximately $35,000. Because of the space limitations, only the first three levels of the workbreakdown structure have been provided. Additional examples of workbreakdown structures and project definitions, using both graphical and tabular methods, are presented in the U. S. Office of Education Cooperative Research Monograph entitled *PERT: Applications in Education* (5).

The importance of developing an adequate project definition or workbreakdown structure cannot be stressed too highly as Archibald and Villoria (1) state:

> This indentured workbreakdown structure is the most important single planning structure, because it establishes the project objectives and provides the framework upon which all the other planning structures can be collated. It is also the basis for project network plans. (p. 28)

An individual first attempting to undertake the workbreakdown structure, or proper definition phase often encounters many problems. One of the major problems centers around a tendency to identify functions and processes rather than work accomplishment or products. In these situations, definitions reflect a concern with the means rather than the ends. The developer of a project definition, while developing the workbreakdown structure, should be concerned with *what* must be done and *why* it is to be done, not *how* it is done. The process step becomes important in identifying the specific tasks that need to be completed in order to reach the "what" and is reflected in the development of the work flow. To persons who are experienced in preparing proposals for federal support, the workbreakdown structure or project definition is similar to the statement of objectives while the process steps are similar to the procedures section.

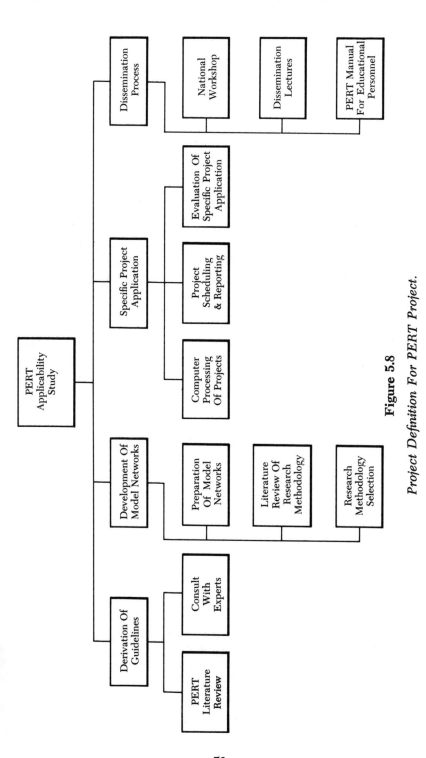

Figure 5.8

Project Definition For PERT Project.

73

Another major problem centers around the beginner's efforts to establish task accomplishment in a time sequence. As a consequence of these efforts, the results of the project definition phase often look like a flow diagram showing movements from the beginning to the end of the project. The workbreakdown structure can reflect this type of sequence to some extent, if it is given a 90 degree turn so that level 0 appears at the right and the higher numbered levels at the left. If this is done, the flow of work necessary to accomplish each of the major objectives can be said to approximate a rough order of sequence. Our experience in developing project definitions has demonstrated that any time sequence is best forgotten while developing the project definition. The developer of a project definition can, if he wants, place within each one of the products at the various levels of the workbreakdown structure, a specific calendar date which will state when he would like to have the product available. Outside of these representations, a time sequence or a calendar is not considered.

The third major problem concerns the developer's ability to be analytical and recognize the major objectives and necessary subobjectives needed to accomplish the major objective. In one sense, the approach to project definition outlined in this chapter represents a new way of thinking for many individuals and requires some time for them to become familiar with the approach as well as the technique. Experience has shown, however, that when persons have become somewhat adept at the technique, they begin to outline many objective activities in this manner.

While the concept of project definition or workbreakdown structure is fairly easy to comprehend, some people find it difficult to actually develop a project definition. There appears to be no satisfactory technique or process by which they can begin the initial efforts to develop a project definition. Figure 5.9 presents a proposed procedure for helping the beginner to start a project definition. It follows a specific to general approach.

First, the mission statement which will outline the basic purpose of the final product of the project is written. The mission statement will list the limits and constraints (time, funding, scope, contractual requirements, agency capabilities, personnel limitations), which will effect the accomplishment of the project.

Second, the tasks or activities that must be accomplished are identified. Not all of the possible tasks can be listed at once since new ones will occur from time to time and can be added to list. Furthermore, the sequence of tasks at this time is not important. It is only important

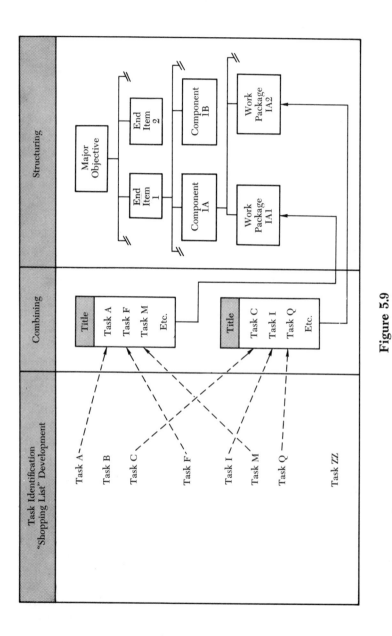

Figure 5.9

Development Of Project Definition–Specific To General.

75

to have a list of them. It might be helpful for this purpose to write each activity that can be foreseen on a small card so that they can be rearranged.

Third, the list or cards prepared from step two are examined and combined into sets of tasks which appear to be related and dependent. Each set of tasks is provided with a title which has a descriptive adjective and noun in it. This title can represent a major project or end item to be produced. It can also be a major or minor function which has to be accomplished. Some combined sets of tasks may be less detailed than others or may even consist of a single task. To some extent, this will depend upon the scope of the work involved.

Fourth, the combined sets of tasks with their identification titles are structured or placed into hierarchical order so that there are at least two sets under a larger grouping, that is the accomplishment of two or more combinations of tasks will lead to the accomplishment of a larger element. We continue combining larger items until the final mission objective is reached or the major end item of the project is identified. This structuring or ordering of tasks should reflect increasing levels of generality. Conversely, lower levels should show increasing detail. After placing together two or more units from the combining phase, this new collection is provided with a label that reflects a product or component, which would be produced as a result of completing the combined sets. The combined sets of tasks at the several levels of the project definition are commonly referred to as *work packages.* Each work package produces some minor or major objective of the project. The term *component* is sometimes used in place of the term, work package. The term becomes secondary to the principle that each component or work package represents a series of lesser tasks combining to produce the objective represented by the package or component.

A common question asked at this point concerns the level of detail that should be shown in a project definition. Unfortunately, no specific criteria exists to indicate at what point the break down should terminate. The problem is further complicated by the fact that a particular component may not need to be subdivided into the same amount of detail as a different component. The number of levels of a project definition becomes a case of wise judgment and experience on the part of the project manager. Attention must be given to the desire of the manager to plan and control the several components. Too little detail means gross components and significant smaller tasks may be overlooked. Too much detail, however, means that time and energy is given to small tasks when these same efforts should be given to larger tasks.

SUMMARY

The essential purpose of the development of the workbreakdown structure, is an attempt to deal with the question of the boundaries of the project. In outlining any system, we always are concerned with what should be included in the system and what should not. The project definition phase is a process step designed to help establish these boundaries. Within the process, the project staff is forced to decide what objectives should be accomplished and how they relate to each other. The interrelationships between sub-objectives and their major objectives will be established more clearly when the project plan is developed. It will then be easily seen that the output resulting from the accomplishment of one or more sub-objectives is the input for the accomplishment of another objective.

It is important to realize that several reviews may have to be made in developing a project definition which is acceptable to people participating in the project. Even though this may consume some time, it will prove to be valuable since the staff will have agreed upon *what* tasks and objectives have to be accomplished.

Although mentioned earlier, it should be stated again that the levels developed in the project definition phase or workbreakdown structure often correspond roughly to the levels of management in an organization or a project. Therefore they can reflect management reporting and control levels. Top level management usually only needs a summary picture of the project in terms of the major objectives or components to be accomplished. A report presented to top management could consist only of the accomplishment of objectives at levels 1 or 2. Operating levels of management, however, often need more detail about the aspect of the project for which they are responsible. This information can be obtained by outlining the tasks or objectives which are to be accomplished at the lower levels. The reports prepared for these individuals would represent the accomplishment of the objectives at lower levels, say levels 3 or 4.

During the project definition phase there is no concern about the sequence in which the objectives will be accomplished. The only concern about sequence during this phase is related to the levels of the hierarchy that are established. Placing the tasks in the specific sequence in which they have to be accomplished is represented by the work flow to be constructed. The next chapter presents various methods by which the sequence of objectives to be accomplished in a time frame can be represented in a graphical manner.

Check List for Project Definition Phase

The following questions can be used as a guide or checklist for determining whether or not the necessary points have been covered in developing the project definition.

1. Does the mission statement state the general overall purpose of the project and the limits and constraints that relate to the project definition?

2. Have all known limits and constraints within which the project must be concerned been identified?

3. Have major end item subdivisions been checked to insure coverage of all work?

4. Has a check been made to be sure that the emphasis is on work accomplished rather than on function performance?

5. Has a check been made to be sure that individual work packages have discernible start and end points?

6. Have milestone dates been assigned for the start and completion of work packages as desired and also for the completion of major end items?

7. If costs are to be associated with work packages, has a cost and accounting summarization system been developed for this purpose?

8. Has a check been made to insure compatibility between the work-breakdown structure with the proposed and/or required contracted terms?

9. Has a check been made to establish compatibility between the workbreakdown structure and the project or institutional organizational scheme?

10. Has responsibility within the organization been assigned to an individual for the development and carry out of work packages?

11. Is the workbreakdown structure that has been developed consistent with the project proposal if the latter is available?

References

1. Archibald, R. D., and R. L. Villoria, *Network-Based Management Systems.* New York: John Wiley & Sons, Inc., 1967, Chapter 2.
2. Avots, Ivars, "Beyond PERT: Precedence Networks," *The MBA,* Vol. II (December, 1967), pp. 46-50.
3. Baumgartner, J. S., *Project Management.* Homewood, Ill.: Richard D. Irwin, Inc., 1963, Chapter 2.
4. Cook, D. L., *Better Project Planning Through System Analysis and Management Techniques.* Columbus, Ohio: Educational Project Management Center, Ohio State University, 1967.
5. _____, *PERT: Applications In Education.* Cooperative Research Monograph Number 17, U. S. Office of Education, 1966, Chapter 2.
6. _____, "The Use of Systems Analyses and Management Systems in Project Planning and Evaluation," *Socio-Economic Planning Sciences,* II, No. 2, 3, 4 (April, 1969), pp. 389-97.
7. Emery, J. C., "The Planning Process and Its Formalization in Computer Models," in *Second Congress on the Information Sciences,* J. Spiegel and D. E. Walker (eds.), Washington, D. C.: Spartan Books, 1965.
8. Granger, C. H., "The Hierarchy of Objectives," *Harvard Business Review,* Vol. XLI (May-June 1964), pp. 63-74.
9. *Handbook for PERT and Companion Cost System.* National Aeronautics and Space Administration (October 30, 1962), Section III.
10. Huggins, W. H., Charles D. Flagle, and Robert Ray, "Flow Graph Representation of Systems" *Operations Research and Systems Engineering,* Baltimore, Md.: John Hopkins Press, 1960, pp. 609-36.

11. *PERT . . . Guide for Management Use.* Washington, D.C.: U. S. Department of Defense, 1963, Chapter 2.

12. *Program Evaluation and Review Technique (PERT).* AMC Regulation 11-29, Washington, D. C.: U. S. Army Material Command Headquarters, June 1966.

13. Starr, M. K. *Production Management Systems and Synthesis.* Englewood Cliffs, N.J.: Prentice-Hall Inc., 1964, pp. iii-vi.

14. Woodgate, H. S., *The Planning Network as a Basis for Resource Allocation, Cost, Planning and Project Profitability Assessment.* London, England: Management Systems Department, International Computers and Tabulators Ltd., 1967.

chapter 6

Developing Project Work Flow

Chapter 5 outlined a procedure for determining the major mission and objectives of the project, the identification of major end items, and the establishment of a hierarchically ordered set of work packages which must be accomplished to reach the final project objective. We were primarily concerned with the identification of *what* had to be done and *why* it was done. To help us with this identification, we used the general concept of a system as a hierarchically ordered set of tasks.

This chapter will begin to develop, for the output of the project definition phase, an order or sequence for the tasks that must be accomplished before reaching the final objective of the project. The primary emphasis, therefore, will be upon *when* the various tasks identified in the project definition must be accomplished. In this chapter we will use a second concept of systems theory, that of representing a system by a flow graph (7). Before discussing the procedure for developing the work plan or flow using this system principle, there are several considerations which should be described as background.

Some Factors in Work Flow Planning

The graphical representation of the actual work flow can take several forms depending on the type of program or project planned. Some of the common forms of representation such as bar charts, milestone charts, and networks, were illustrated in Chapter 4. The form of representation will be decided by the nature of the project, whether or not it is *deterministic* or *probabilistic*.

Projects involving the construction of a school building are largely deterministic since there is a great deal of information on how the work flow proceeds. A bar chart might be a good technique to use in representing the work flow since it would serve management purposes in an effective way. A research and development project might well be considered probabilistic since there is either limited or no knowledge on how work flow should proceed. Under these circumstances, the use of a network representing the work flow might be appropriate since networks are considered more flexible and dynamic. They are usually considered more suitable for outlining the work flow in situations which will probably change in moving from initiation to completion.

Each graphical representation procedure has its own set of principles and rules for construction and use. Each requires the potential user to develop a familiarity with these principles and rules before using them. If the user is at least familiar with the technique, problems of understanding it will not hinder its implementation in a given situation. Frequently many applications of network techniques fail simply because the individuals applying them have not taken the time to study the techniques before utilizing them in a given situation.

No matter which graphical representation procedure is employed to represent the work flow, the developed work plan will serve several functions (15). It will be a logical expression of the project plan. It will serve to show visually the logic that underlies the method of accomplishing the movement from initiation to completion. A graphic plan will expose the logic involved in it, and others may comment upon and perhaps even challenge it. Still, the graphical plan is physical evidence that a plan does exist even though it may not be the best one. Furthermore, the plan can serve as a communication tool. Presentation of the work flow by means of a graphical diagram can show an uninformed person how the project will be completed more easily than many pages of written description. If the plan is large enough, it can be placed in a central location so that the whole project staff may see how work is progressing as well as the individual responsibilities for the accomplishment of tasks. Graphical representation can also provide a basis for control once the project is under way. Progress in the form of completed tasks can be marked directly on the chart. Delays can be noticed more readily. Marking progress in this manner can provide the project staff with a feeling of accomplishment and movement toward the objective.

The development of the work flow should involve as many of the individuals who are or will be involved in the actual completion of the project as possible. It is also important while developing the work plan to involve the personnel who will do the tasks. Under this procedure, there may be a greater commitment to the work than there is when the plan is simply imposed upon the personnel who have not been involved in planning the work they are expected to carry out. This is not always possible in projects where many of the personnel will not become involved before the project is funded. In these cases, the initiator of the project might develop preliminary plans and then subject them to revision once the necessary personnel are available and working on the project. In general, an outline of the plan using major end items from the project definition phase could be developed by the top level management of the project. This brief outline then would serve as a guidance document for planning at the lower levels of the project staff. Regardless of the level of management involved, the planning group should consist of a small number of persons, no more than three or four at the most, in order to avoid the difficulties of personal interests and conflicts often associated with large groups. The efforts of the small planning group can be presented later to the larger group for suggestions and revision.

The output of the work flow step will be some type document which will portray in a graphic manner the interdependency and interrelationship of the tasks that must be done. The graphic plan developed may be relatively small in size or it may cover an entire wall. The size will vary in terms of the amount of detail shown and the complexity of the operation. As in the project definition phase, no explicit criteria can be given about the size of the work flow phase. The management's desire for detail, the size of the project, and other similar variables have to be considered in developing the actual representation.

In this chapter, primary emphasis will be given to representing project work flow by the use of network techniques. This does not mean that the other techniques are not valuable. They are and should be used when they are appropriate. Since their initial development in the late 1950's, networks have been found to be highly useful ways of representing work flows, particularly because they require the interrelationships and dependencies of the tasks to be more firmly established than the other techniques. Often individuals have reported that simply drawing a network with no further implementation of the management system has enabled them to see the work flow and its logic in a manner that had not been apparent to them previously. Networking techniques are empasized also because of their relative newness and because many individuals in the field of education are unfamiliar with them. Furthermore, networking concepts are useful in introducing individuals who are not familiar with general systems concepts to some of the selected concepts of systems.

The Concept of a Flow Graph

In Chapter 5, we defined the project as a system. Systems can be demonstrated or represented in various forms. Mathematical formulations and visual representations are two ways of representing a system. A visual representation is a more appropriate technique for our situation since the result of its application is a graphical representation.

Diagrammatic representation in which flow through the system is portrayed by a sequence of unidirected arrows is called a *flow graph.* The unidirectional arrows, which usually go from left to right, are called *arcs.* The beginning and end of each of these arcs is marked off usually with circles called *nodes.* One or more arcs may lead into and out of a given node. Figure 6.1 illustrates a simple arc-node pattern.

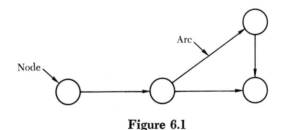

Figure 6.1

Simple Arc-node Pattern.

Networking techniques employ the basic concepts of *arc* and *node* from flow graph methodology. However, in the network technique, their names are changed to *activities* and *events.*

The more common types of networking procedures are relatively recent. The three most common types are Program Evaluation and Review Technique (PERT), Critical Path Method (CPM), and precedence diagramming. Each employs the basic pattern of network representation but each differs slightly in its operational characteristics and application. The balance of this chapter will be devoted to discussing some of the basic concepts of networking, presenting general rules and principles of construction, and illustrating various modes of constructing a network representation of work plans.

Basic Networking Concepts or Language

There are four basic concepts in networking techniques which are fundamental to further work. These concepts are *network, activity, event,* and *constraint.*

Network. The network is a graphical representation of all the tasks or jobs that must be accomplished to reach the several intermediate and final objectives of the project. It will show the planned sequence of accomplishment and the interdependency and interrelationship of the tasks. Networks may be rather general in detail or very detailed, showing the tasks that have to be done. Flow in the network is always considered unidirectional, going from left to right. It should be realized that the sequence of tasks represented in the network might be seen differently by individuals with different ideas of how the work flow should proceed. These differences in work flow can represent alternative sets of work tasks for accomplishing the project. A consideration of the alternative sets of work tasks could be the subject of staff meetings. After considering the possible alternatives, a final network should be agreed upon and adopted for use by the project staff. Figure 6.2 presents an illustration of a simple network.

Activity. Activities are the individual tasks or jobs which must be done to reach an objective. An activity represents both the time and work effort needed to accomplish a objective. Consequently, an activity is said to consume both time and resources. Activities may represent a process, a task, a period of waiting, mental or physical work, a constraint, or a combination of these things. The accomplishment of an activity should represent the accomplishment of a task in the total hierarchy of work outlined in the project definition phase. A given activity in a network can present a task which is long or short in duration, a general task or a detailed task.

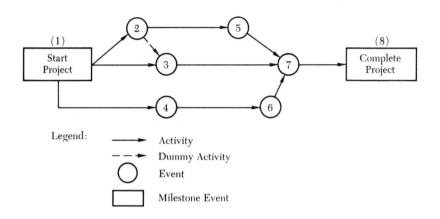

Legend:
→ Activity
-- → Dummy Activity
○ Event
▭ Milestone Event

Figure 6.2

Illustration Of Simple Network.

One of the major problems in an activity is to define it in such a manner that estimates of the time needed to complete it can be obtained in later phases of planning. This problem requires that careful attention be given to the exact nature of the job. An activity such as "reviewing literature" presents no explicit statement of what and how much literature should be reviewed. Until this statement is made, we cannot decide when the task is completed or estimate the time needed to complete it.

Activities are usually described in a type of telegraphic language which identifies the action to be taken and the end product to be developed. For example, "develop tryout questionnaire," "employ research staff," "conduct item analysis" might be activity descriptions. In each description there is an active verb as well as an adjective and noun which helps to clarify the specific task to be done. These abbreviated statements can be expanded by supplemental descriptions which will indicate more precisely the nature of the task.

An activity is usually represented on the network by a solid arrow line (———→) such as the one shown in Figure 6.2. To facilitate drawing the network, there is no connection between the length of the activity arrow and the time to do the job. A short term activity may be represented by a long arrow line while a long term task can be represented by a much shorter line. This procedure enables us to draw the network without a particular time frame. Some networks are drawn, however, so that the actual length of the line corresponds to the time needed for the job. These networks are called *time-scaled* networks. The beginner in network construction should avoid time phasing the network so that he can feel free to draw the activity arrows as they are needed in order to show the sequence of tasks in their proper order.

Events. Events represent *points* of accomplishment in the network. Consequently, they do not consume either time or resources. An event usually represents the start or end of an activity. An event either exists or does not exist since it must represent a clearly definable point of occurrence. Events are labeled with terms such as "start" or "complete," "begin" or "end," or any other set of words that denotes the initiation or completion of work. An event cannot occur until every activity and event preceding it has been accomplished, and activities and events following a given event cannot start until the event has occurred.

Events are usually represented on the network by a geometric figure such as the circle shown in Figure 6.2. In contrast to activities, there are specific designations used in certain types of events. The most common types of special events are *milestone* and *interface* events.

Milestone events usually represent the accomplishment of a major piece of work such as the accomplishment of a work package or a major objective. These events are usually designated by top level management. Consequently, progress reports forwarded to the higher levels of management may reflect only the status of the event's accomplishment. Milestone events are distinguished from regular events by special symbols such as squares or rectangles.

An interface event occurs when two separate networks or sub-networks within a larger network possess an event which is common to both of them. An interface event might represent the availability, at a particular point in time, of information from one network which is needed to move ahead in another network. These events are represented by a geometric figure, such as a triangle, in order to easily distinguish them from regular and milestone events.

Events must be carefully labeled. Illustrative event labels might be "start questionnaire mailing," "item analysis completed," "project approved" and "begin data analysis." Like activities, they must be labeled in a manner that all individuals on the project staff understand. The project staff must know their meaning and be able to determine if the event has taken place. It is difficult to give only one label to a particular event because it may represent the completion or start of one or more activities. The final decision for labeling is made by the management. It may be more important to note the completion of an activity than the start of a subsequent activity. A given event circle can present the start and completion of more than one activity. Even though the event is given only one label, it must be interpreted in terms of the start and completion of all activities leading into and out of it.

Constraint and Dependency. The concepts of constraint and dependency are important to developing a work flow and should be fully understood. Constraint means that a given activity may not start until the preceding activity has been completed. A succeeding activity, however, cannot be begun until its preceeding event has been reached. For example, we would say that activity A is a constraint upon activity B which follows activity A.

In establishing or drawing the work plan, the activities that logically constrain other activities or tasks first must be determined. A great deal of time and thought is given in the initial planning to determining the constraints. If the constraints are not determined early in the planning phase, there may be problems in accomplishing the proper sequence of work.

Sometimes, there is one activity which serves as a logical constraint upon another activity but not because the work must be accomplished before the other activity can be begun. For example, one activity might produce a document which is needed in another part of the project. In this situation, the document serves as a constraint upon further work in that part of the project. To show this type of constraint, a concept known as the "dummy activity" is employed, and a dotted line (----------→) as shown in Figure 6.2 usually represents the con-.straint.

Dummy activities do not consume time or resources. They are em-·ployed to show dependencies and constraints that exist within the total project effort. Constraints, however, are not solely represented by the dummy activity lines. Normal activities can and do serve as constraints upon each other. The dummy activity line is a vehicle which allows us to show certain constraints that do not involve time or resources. Figures 6.3, 6.4, and 6.5 illustrate the constraints that exist in certain situations.

In Figure 6.3, activity A is bound by the events 1 and 2 and constrains any movement to initiate activity B bound by events 2 and 3. We could also say that activity B is constrained by the completion of activity A or is dependent upon the completion of activity A.

Figure 6.4 exhibits a more complex set of constraints. The completion of activities, A, B, and C, serve as a constraint upon movement on

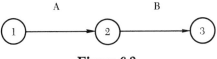

Figure 6.3

Illustration Of A Simple Constraint.

activity D. All three of these activities must be completed, even though they may occur at different times, before event 4 can take place and work on activity D begin.

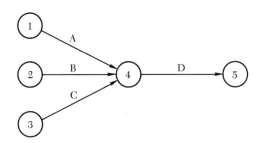

Figure 6.4

Illustration Of A Complex Constraint.

There are occasions when a constraint exists between selected portions of a total project and should be considered. Figure 6.5 illustrates a case in which completion of a task in one work flow or network path must occur before movement can take place in another work flow. Since no actual time is consumed we can employ the dummy activity to show this constraint.

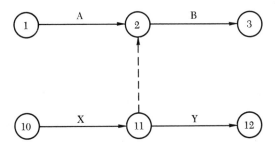

Figure 6.5

Illustration Of Dummy Activity To Show Constraint.

In the illustration, activity X must be completed before activity B can be begun. It should be noted, however, that both activities A and X constrain movement on activities B and Y.

Many individuals just beginning to develop skill in network theory are confused by dummy activities. They seem to feel that it is the only method of showing constraint in a work plan. It is not. The dummy activity provides a convenient means of showing constraint between parts of the network, particularly when one task must be done before another can begin. It should be remembered that normal or regular activities also can serve as constraints.

Principles and Procedures

The basic principle in network construction is the observance of the constraint relationship. In addition to this specific rule or principle, there are other rules or principles which must be observed in developing the network. Some of these rules are the result of utilizing the computer for processing network data, particularly in the time and cost phases.

First, any event in the network must be unique in that it appears only once in the network.

Second, activities in a network are independent of each other. That is, the time that one activity takes does not effect the time that another activity in the network takes. Each stands alone and by itself.

Third, only one activity can exist between any pairs of events. This rule is illustrated in Figure 6.6 where we see that there are two

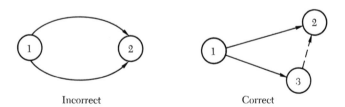

Incorrect   Correct

Figure 6.6

Illustration Of Unique Event Rule.

activities A and B existing between event numbers 1 and 2. Under the rules of networking this is not permissible. We can correct the situation by using a dummy activity line. As corrected, the activity meets the criteria explicit in the rule. This rule insures that the proper identification of the activities can be made by utilizing their preceding and succeeding event numbers during computer processing.

Fourth, there should be no *loops* in the network. Looping consists of developing endless circles in the network as illustrated in Figure 6.7.

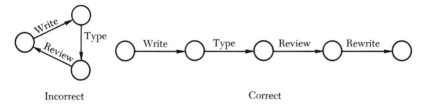

Incorrect   Correct

Figure 6.7

Illustration Of Network Loop.

Here we can see that having reached an event we move into a subsequent activity which eventually returns us to the same event that was formerly completed. We can correct the situation by reconstructing the sequence of events and activities.

Various authors and references on PERT present some minor variations in the principles and rules of network construction, but these present the basic guidelines which should be followed. Within the basic concepts presented earlier and utilizing the rules and principles we have outlined let us now turn to procedures for the actual construction of a network.

Procedures for Network or Work Plan Construction

Frustration often results in initial efforts to draw a network, even when the general approaches to network construction have been described. When faced with the actual task of construction, individuals ask, "Where do I begin?" and "How do I start?" Each constructor appears to have his particular method of approach to the problem. When a project is particularly large, individuals find it difficult to fully comprehend all that should be included. Regardless of the size of the project, the project definition phase is used as the primary basis for network costruction, moving either from a general to specific case or from a specific to general case. Each of these approaches will be described in this chapter.

Let us turn first to the situation of moving from the specific to the general. This approach is illustrated in Figure 6.8. Once the project

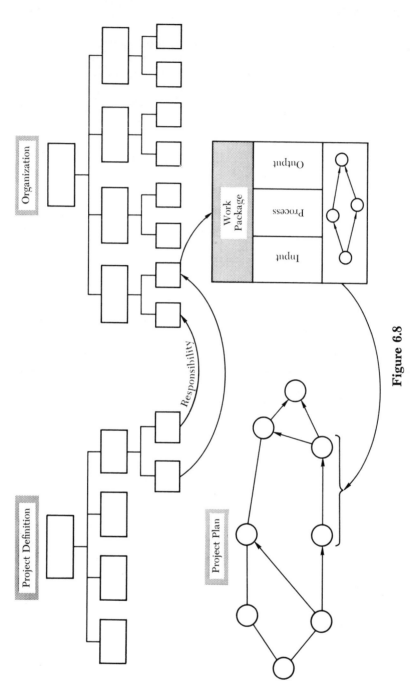

Figure 6.8

Specific To General Procedure For Network Construction.

WORK SHEET

Sub-Unit: *Perceptions & Conceptual Design*   Responsibility: *C. Achilles*

Work Task: *Develop Instrument Drafts*

Input	Sequence or Process Steps	Output
Time Constraints	015-022 Dummy Activity	
Data Needs	016-017 Study Lit. to Revise Instrum.	
Lit. on Theory	017-018 Develop Format	
and Design	017-019 Obtain Large Pool of Items	
Consultant Help in	018-022 Write General Instructions	
A. Instrumentation	019-020 Reduce Pool of Items	
B. Validation	020-015 Test Item Discrimination	
PL88-210	020-022 Test Item Validity	
Previous Decisions	022-023 Write Preliminary Draft	
	023-024 Critique Draft	
	024-025 Re-Draft	
		Drafts of
		Instrument

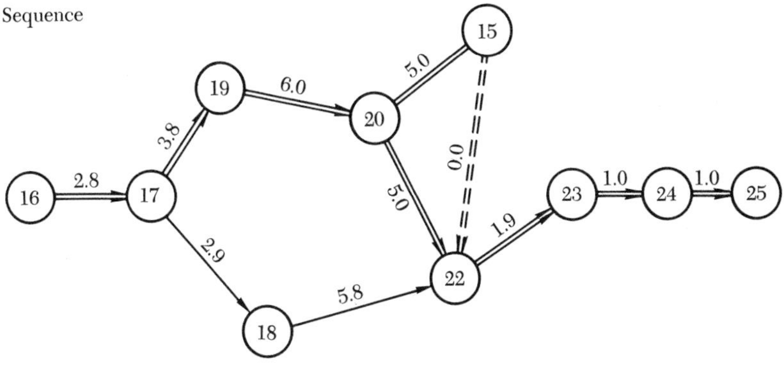

Approval _____ Date _____

Figure 6.9

Illustration Of Work Package Work Sheet. (Reproduced from
A Nationwide Study of the Administration of Vocational–Tech-
nical Education at the State Level, *Project No. 6-2921, Contract
No. OEG -4-6-000542-0001, August, 1967, School of Education,
University of California, Berkeley, California.)*

definition has been completed, various work packages or elements of the project definition phase are assigned to units or departments of the organization to develop into a network. This is done for two reasons. First, it is more than likely that organizational units will be responsible for accomplishing the work package and, therefore, should participate in its development. Second, functional departments often have the expertise and knowledge about how a particular task should be accomplished. Assigning work packages in this manner will make more effective use of these personnel.

Once the work package is assigned to a department or departments it is developed, using the work sheet shown in Figure 6.9. Here we identify the title of the work package and the person responsible for its development. The work sheet is divided into three principal components; an input section, a process section, and an output section. In completing the work sheet, needed information, material, and necessary decisions and known constraints are listed in the input column. Then the various steps or tasks that have to be done to accomplish the work package are outlined, but not necessarily in order of their accomplishment. Each of these steps will be equivalent to an activity.

The particular item of information, product, or decision which will be the result of the work done in the process steps is listed in the output column. Once the three columns are completed, the process steps are drawn at the bottom of the chart in their logical sequence to show the work flow for the work package. When all the work packages have been developed, they are combined into a larger network showing the total project plan as illustrated in Figure 6.8.

There is a strong correspondence between the project definition and the work plan. An individual should be able to examine a project definition and find a particular work package, or a series of work packages on the network. Conversely, he should be able to examine a network and find some corresponding work packages in the project definition phase. In this approach, the responsibility for work package development is at the lowest operating level of the organization, and consolidation occurs towards the upper levels of management.

In contrast to the specific to general procedure, the network can be constructed through a general to specific procedure. In this process the first step is the development of a summary network, using the major elements of the first and second levels of the workbreakdown structure to identify major milestone events and large activities which represent work packages. Referring again to Figure 6.8, we would proceed from the project definition to the network figure which appears at the bottom left. Once the major milestone events and general activities are laid out, the activities can be assigned to organizational units for further elaboration, utilizing the same work sheet exhibited in the specific to general procedure. The general to specific procedure is appropriate in a large project. In this situation, the central planning staff might undertake a project definition followed by the master or summary network in order to have a guidance document for the rest of the participating units and personnel who will outline their specific tasks.

In addition to the two approaches we have described, many writers discuss forward and backward approaches. Of these approaches, the backward approach is more recommended. The initial step in the backward approach is the identification of the major end item or event of the project. After this step, the writer proceeds backwards, asking the question "What events must be done in order to reach this event?" During this process, the activities and events are laid out backwards to reach the eventual starting point. The forward approach begins by asking the questions "What must we do first?" followed by questions which generate subsequent activities that lead to the final event. Network constructors favoring the backwards approach claim that it is more likely to generate a network that will contain only the events and activities which must be achieved to reach the final objective rather than every possible activity. It is their contention that the forward approach leads to a idealistic rather than practical network. Some writers on network construction have even suggested starting in the middle and moving out in either direction.

Regardless of the particular approach used, the primary objective is to form a logical, realistic, valid, and graphical representation of the tasks and events that must be accomplished in order to complete the project. To accomplish this task we should keep in mind several guiding questions. If our concern is primarily with events, we might ask questions such as "What events must occur before this one can occur?" and "What events can occur after this one?" If our concern is with activities, then we might ask questions such as "What activities must occur before this activity can occur?" or "What activities can occur after this one is completed?" and "What activities can go on concurrently or parallel to another activity?" These questions and others help to check the logic of the work plan. Questions such as "Must I do this before I do that?" or "Can this go on at the same time that another job is going on?" are typical of logic questioning.

Practical Aspects of Network Construction

The preceding section described generalized procedures for work flow development. The actual job of developing a work plan, however, has some practical dimensions which must be considered. A common question raised by beginners concerns the amount of detail that should exist in a network. This question does not have a definite answer since the amount of detail depends upon the size and complexity of the project, the degree of uncertainty existing in the task, and familiarity with the work to be performed. Obviously, an activity such as putting stamps on a questionnaire would not be included since it is a rather detailed task. If, however, it is an important task in the project, it should appear as an integral part of a network. Perhaps the best solution is to develop the detail deemed necessary by the project manager for proper planning and controlling of the project. Some individuals can manage the project successfully with general details while others require more specific details.

Sometimes there is confusion about the appropriate labels for events or identifying activities on the network. In some cases, circles turn out to represent activities rather than the arrow lines. In this case, the individual has developed a precedence diagram rather than a network diagram although they are similar in appearance. In order to maintain clarity, at least upon the initial drawing of the network, a description of the task to be done should be actually written down on the arrow line. This forces the constructor to remember the nature of an activity rather than an event. Once a network is finalized, the constructor can label events in a manner that he feels is best for proper planning and control of the project and communication with the staff.

Early efforts in drawing a network should be done on a blackboard, or on pieces of paper such as flip charts, wrapping paper, or newsprint, using pencils and erasers. Once a network is drawn and accepted by the staff, a draftsman can reproduce it in a more formal form. Most of the networks presented in publications have gone through a similar process and were not developed in formal format right from the start. Drawing the network and maintaining it during the course of a project can be handled well on a large piece of wall board or room wall by placing a glassene over the cardboard and drawing the network upon it, using a grease pencil. Under this procedure, it is easy to modify the drawing when it is necessary.

Large and detailed networks are hard to comprehend particularly by others who have not been involved in their construction. The establishment of *sub-networks* can help to reduce large and detailed networks to managable units. Sub-networks can represent activities shown on the large network. Event numbers show where the sub-networks fit into the large network. It should be remembered that the more detailed the network, the more difficult it is to change during the course of the project. The use of sub-networks makes it easier to introduce changes since only the sub-network may need to be changed and not the detail that appears in the large network.

In the original development of network techniques, it was anticipated that the data generated within the network would be processed by computers. Consequently, events are usually given numbers. Numbering schemes vary from user to user, but the two major numbering schemes are *sequential* and *random*. In sequential numbering, events are numbered from left to right running concurrently to the terminal event. Under random numbering, events are numbered in a nonsystematic manner. In this procedure, a large number may appear at the beginning or middle of the network and a small number at the end. Random numbering procedures should be employed in numbering events as sequential numbering systems may become disrupted if new events and activities are inserted. Most computer programs will take either types of numbers but experience has demonstrated that random numbering is the preferred method. A series of events which make up a particular work package should receive a set of numbers which are particular to a given work package or end item. For example, all events associated with the development of a questionnaire might be numbered 100–199, while all events associated with the analysis of data might be numbered 500–599. Using blocks of numbers enables the constructor to quickly identify an activity or event associated with a particular dimension of the project.

The event numbers can be used to describe the work tasks in a network. For example, a network can be drawn showing only the numbers of the activities and events and listing underneath activity or event descriptions. If the list consists of activities, then it will show both preceding and succeeding numbers as well as an activity description. Or, the list might be made up of events. In this instance, only a single number is listed as well as a description of the event using the start and complete language. This procedure permits networks to be drawn on a relatively small scale as long as the reader has a list of activities or events so that he can identify them.

It is helpful in constructing networks to make no assumptions about the length of an activity line and the time needed to do a particular job. A long activity line might represent a short period of time while a short line may represent a long period of time. Utilizing this assumption, it is easy to draw networks. The network constructor, however, may choose to have the activity line represent the actual time for the job. When these networks are developed, they are referred to as *time-scaled* networks. Sometimes this procedure results in a long chart since the time scale must be maintained for perhaps a three or four year period.

One of the common questions asked by the beginner in networking concerns the projects of long duration. Should these projects be drawn in detail in the initial planning efforts? The answer is generally no. It is perfectly permissible to develop only an early portion of the network, for example the first year, in detail. The succeeding second, third, and fourth years can be drawn in less detail in the initial planning effort. This procedure is possible because we are not sure what will be the progress of the project, and therefore cannot make a detailed commitment. However, as we approach the end of the first year, we should begin to detail the second year and perhaps provide additional detail for the third and fourth years. This method of increasing the detail as we progress enables us to deal with uncertain research and development efforts. It also provides an opportunity for revision as work progresses. Furthermore, people are likely to find the network more acceptable, particularly if they do not want to make a commitment to great detail early in the project.

Another problem which frequently arises is only related to network construction. Many people feel that the development of the initial network to show work flow commits them to following this network forever. They should realize that the network simply reflects the way that a person plans or anticipates proceedings to progress. It is, therefore, a reflection of the sequence developed by some individual or group. Should the group change its mind, it can modify the network accordingly. In fact, it is more likely that the network will change to reflect modifications in work plans than remain stable. Should a situation arise in which the network is used to lock people into accomplishing a task, then it is being used improperly by the project manager.

Types of Networks

Until now, the discussion has focused on network construction in general. There are many types of networks which can be developed to reflect the various concerns of management. This section will discuss some of the more common types of networks.

Event or Activity Oriented Networks. Some networks are referred to as event-oriented or activity-oriented networks. In event-oriented networks, the primary concern is the occurrence of events. The identification of events and the order of their occurence receives the principal emphasis. PERT is an event-oriented system. Most of the time calculations that are developed for management relate directly to events. An activity-oriented network concerns the description and flow of activities rather than their beginning and end. These networks are most often found in discussion of CPM (Critical Path Method). To some extent, these two types of networks reflect the deterministic and probabilistic situations previously noted. Because of the uncertainty associated with some activities, the principal concern in some networks is the time of an event's occurence. In some construction activities, however, the principal concern is outlining the sequence of jobs that must be done, and there is less concern about uncertainty or probability dimensions.

Functional or Banded Networks. Another common type of network is the function or banded network. In these networks, activities and events are shown in groupings which represent the organizational responsibility for a given set of tasks, or work associated with a major dimension of a project. A simplified example of the banded network is presented in Figure 6.10. This network actually represents a condensation of larger network designed to show the steps involved in developing a junior college as outlined by Benson (2). At the left side of the network, the major organizational units which are responsible for total development are shown. The work going on between these units can be shown by the use of interface events in the network.

Summary Network. A third type of network is a summary network, in contrast to a detailed or operating network. In the summery network, major activities and events as well as milestone and interface events are exhibited. These networks are prepared for higher levels of management since their prime concern is only with the completion of major jobs. Operating or detailed networks are developed at lower levels of management for day-to-day use. When summary networks are developed from detailed networks, the identification of events and activities during progress must be maintained in the summary network. A similar relationship between levels and sections of networks is shown in Figure 6.11. This figure was adapted from that provided by Woodgate in his text on network planning and shows that a particular event or activity can be traced from a summary high

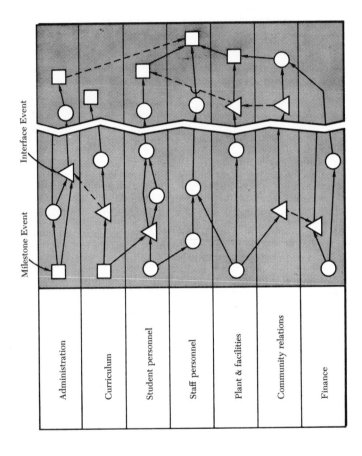

Figure 6.10

Illustration Of A Banded Or Functional Network.

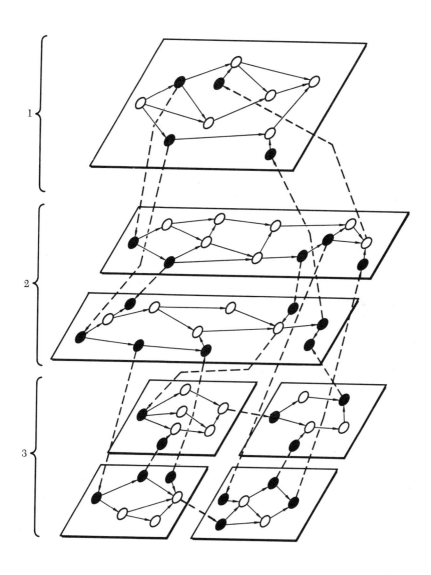

Figure 6.11

Illustration Of Multi-Level And Sectionalized Networks.
(*Adapted from H. S. Woodgate,* Planning by Network, *Brandon Systems Press, 1967.*)

level management network to a network developed for a sub-unit or function department at the operating level.

Master Network. In contrast, the master network exhibits all of the events and activities making up the total project network. The master network is detailed and may provide a listing of all events and activities, not only the on-going operations but also the tasks that have been completed. Computers are often used as a means of storing this large amount of information about the network. By this means, a history of how the project was accomplished can be provided which will list all activities and events involved during the project.

Model Network. A fifth type of network is a model or standardized network. In these cases, certain processes or tasks have been performed in the past, thus permitting the identification of a particular process with some certainty. Many business and industrial concerns have these standardized or model networks. When a new project is developed, model or standardized networks are incorporated into the total network under construction. For example, it would be possible to outline the steps for the construction of an opinion scale or an achievement test so that any project that involved these same activities could use this network. It is encouraging to note that these networks are becoming available to the field of education for many processes. Illustrations of several model networks appear in the author's monograph on PERT published by the U. S. Office of Education (3).

Colored Network. Another type of network is referred to as a colored network. In these networks, different colors are used to portray different organizational responsibilities for the various activities and events. One network developed by a state department of education involves the local school district, the state department guidance office and a data processing division. The activities associated with the school are shown in one color, those associated with the guidance department in another, and the data processing ones in a third color. This type of network enables the staff to see their responsibility for performing certain tasks as well as when participation is required by a particular organizational unit.

Precedence Diagramming. In Chapter 4, reference was made to "precedence diagramming." This concept was illustrated in Figure 4.3 as an alternative procedure to the network techniques employed in PERT and CPM. In appearance, precedence diagramming is very similar to the concepts and principles of networking discussed in this chapter. There are, however, some differences between typical network procedures and precedence diagramming. Perhaps the most salient difference is that activities are actually represented with circles or nodes rather than arrow lines. In turn, the arrow lines serve to connect the various activities or nodes. For this reason, precedence diagramming is sometimes referred to as the "Activity-on-the-node" approach to drawing networks. In normal networking procedures, time is assigned to the arrow line, but in precedence diagramming the time is recorded in the circle. Normal network time calculations can be made under this procedure.

Precedence diagramming has certain advantages, particularly for the person newly initiated in networking. First, it is easy to understand. Furthermore, it eliminates many, if not all, of the dummy activities which may appear in a regular network. It also simplifies interpretation because events and their sometimes confusing descriptions and interpretations are eliminated. It can reduce the number of activities which would exist in a regular network.

It does have some disadvantages of which the reader must be aware. Events that are important to the successful completion of a project are frequently eliminated. This is particularly true in the case of milestone and interface events. It is not possible to integrate these networks through the use of interface events. Furthermore, these diagrams need specialized computer programs to process them and, therefore, are not often used. Finally, finding a critical path through the precedence diagram is often difficult since the event number linkage is missing.

Precedence diagramming is most frequently used in the construction trades which are usually completely activity-oriented. Once normal networking is understood and the basic rules and principles grasped, it is just as easy to work with as precedence diagramming.

Summary

This chapter has presented the general rules and principles for constructing a work flow or plan for the project as a second step in the planning sub-system. There is a strong relationship between the first phase of planning, that of project definition, and the second, that of developing the work flow. The chapter emphasized the utilization of network concepts as a means of representing work plans. This emphasis does not mean that it is the only way to represent work plans. There are a variety of techniques for doing so. Our principal concern is that some graphical device is established to show the work flow in order to properly manage the effort. Network techniques have been successful and therefore have been emphasized.

Once the work plan has been developed, and it may take several revisions before arriving at a plan acceptable to the project staff, it is possible to move on to the third major activity in the planning subsystem, that of developing a time frame for the project. The next chapter is devoted to the concepts, principles, and rules of developing time frames for a work flow.

Check List for Project Work Flow

Listed below are several questions which can be used as a check list for making sure that the necessary actions have been covered in developing the project work flow before entering into the time estimation phase.

1. Has a master work flow been developed from the project definition which shows the general project plan?

2. Are the sub-networks and detailed networks developed consistently with the master work plan?

3. Is it possible to relate the activities and tasks on the detailed networks to the overall or master work plan?

4. Have events or start and completion points been checked for uniqueness (i.e., do they occur only once in the work plan)?

5. Has the work plan or network been checked for possible "loops"?

6. Has each activity or task been identified with the unique set of preceding and succeeding event numbers?

7. Have the interfaces between sub-networks or work plans been identified and marked appropriately?

8. Have major milestone events been identified and designated?

9. Has some form of an event numbering system been adopted?

10. Has the preliminary project work flow been approved by the appropriate and necessary levels of project management?

References

1. Archibald, R. D. and R. L. Villoria, *Network Based Management Systems*. New York: John Wiley & Sons, 1967, Chapter 3 and Appendix B.
2. Benson, Ellis, *A Time and Sequence Analysis of Critical Steps In The Establishment of California Junior Colleges*, Ph.D. Dissertation, University of California at Los Angeles, 1963.
3. Cook, Desmond L., *PERT: Applications in Education*. Cooperative Research Monograph Number 17, U. S. Office of Education, 1966.
4. _____, "The Use of Systems Analysis and Management Systems in Project Planning and Evaluation," *Socio-Economic Planning Sciences*, II, No. 2, 3, 4 (April, 1969), pp. 389-97.
5. Dean, K. L., *Fundamentals of Network Planning and Analysis*. UNIVAC Division, Sperry Rand Corporation, 1962.
6. Hopeman, Richard J., *Systems Analysis and Operations Management*. Columbus, Ohio: Charles E. Merrill Publishing Co., 1969.
7. Huggins, W. H., Charles D. Flagle, and Robert Ray, "Flow Graph Representation of Systems," *Operations Research and Systems Enginering*, Baltimore, Md.: John Hopkins University Press, 1960, pp. 609-36.
8. Malcolm, D. G., J. H. Roseboom, C. E. Clark, and W. Fazar, "Application of a Technique for Research and Development Program Evaluation," *Operations Research*, Vol. VII (September 1959), pp. 646-69.
9. *PERT Fundamentals*, "Volume I—Networking", Washington, D.C.: U. S. Government Printing Office.
10. *PERT . . . Guide for Management Use*. PERT Coordinating Group, Department of Defense, Washington, D. C.

11. *Planning and Scheduling with PERT and CPM.* Newburyport, Massachusetts: Entelek Inc., 1964.
12. Reninger, Normand W., *A Study of the Network Concept of Planning Complex Projects,* Master's thesis, Columbus, Ohio: Ohio State University, 1962.
13. Sagan, Edgar L., *A Network Model For Planning and Establishing Higher Education Consortiums,* Unpublished Doctoral Dissertation, Columbus, Ohio: Ohio State University, 1969.
14. Stires, D. M., and M. M. Murphy, *Modern Management Methods— PERT and CPM.* Boston, Massachusetts: Materials Management Institute, 1964.
15. Woodgate, H. S., *Planning by Network.* London, England: Business Publications Limited, 1964.

chapter 7

Time Estimation Procedure

The third major step in project planning is the development of a time frame for the total project and the individual activities and events within the project. Most operating management systems have emphasized both the planning and controlling of time as the fundamental element for management action. The importance of a time base was recognized by Gantt in his early work and has continued to be emphasized. An examination of the various management systems described in Chapter 4 will reveal some type of time flow or schedule for each one. Time is used as a means of dealing with costs as well as performance.

The initial time estimation phase provides data for the project management information system. The following list presents the specific kinds of information and data generated for use by the project manager.

1. Expected duration of an individual activity or work package.
2. The earliest time a particular event or the total project can be accomplished.
3. The latest allowable time an event can occur and still not delay the project.

4. The critical or most time consuming pathway through the network.

5. The amount of slack or free time that exists within a pathway or is associated with an event or with an activity or in the total project.

The subsequent sections of this chapter will be devoted to the procedures which have been developed within the network systems, particularly probabilistic ones, to generate this planning data and information. But before discussing the concepts and principles there are several basic considerations which must be presented.

First, we must recognize that a degree of uncertainty exists in almost every research and development project. In most cases, there is no background or experience on which to build reasonably certain and confident time, cost, or performance estimates. If this data were available to us as we estimated the time needed to do a job, then the range of our uncertainty would be relatively low, and our confidence would be high. The time estimating procedure must have a means of dealing with this uncertainty.

Second, there are two general types of time estimates: *deterministic* and *probabilistic.* Deterministic estimates become available to us when we have past experience with an individual job, and there is little uncertainty about how long the job will take. In these cases, usually a single estimate will suffice for the particular activity involved. Probabilistic estimates are based upon the fact that uncertainty does exist about a particular activity. All that can be done in this case is to make some reasonably approximate estimate based upon our present view and knowledge of the task. When working with probabilistic estimates, usually two or more estimates rather than only one are obtained. The most common procedure is to secure three estimates as exists in the PERT technique. It is likely that within a given project both deterministic and probabilistic estimates will exist. Some jobs will have a history and, therefore, can be estimated with reasonable certainty. In other cases, the jobs have not been done before, and we will have to resort to probabilistic estimating procedures.

Third, the manager must realize that the time to do a task, job, or activity is a function of the activity itself, and the planned resources that can be applied to that particular activity. Because of this, each activity must be carefully defined. It is not unusual during the course of the project planning stage to revise certain activity descriptions in order to obtain better time estimates. It is assumed that an *effective* resource application will be made. We do not presume an *optimum* resource allocation. We can operate either from planned manpower or actual manpower availability. It is further assumed that these resources will be applied at an average rate which is interpreted as an eight hour day, a forty hour week. When considering the resource problem, assigned schedule dates and competition within the organizational structure for resources are not important. For example, if, in the time we are estimating, a duplicating task is involved, we do not worry about the present work load in the duplicating department. This consideration enters in the actual scheduling of the project. Time estimates obtained after a consideration of the activity and an effective resource application are eventually translated into an actual schedule. The schedule then becomes a part of the data base for the information system.

Some Rules and Procedures

The primary starting point for time estimation is the work packages and activities to be completed. It is important, therefore, that they are well defined and provide a valid basis for the estimates.

Whenever possible the individual providing the estimate should be the same one who will do the work or is most familiar with the task. This is not always possible, particularly in the planning phase, but it is desirable for several reasons. First, requesting time information from people who will participate in the project helps to involve them in the work of the project. Second, the individual who has done similar tasks in the past will be more aware of pitfalls, problems, and related concerns than the individual with no experience in the activity. The person providing the estimate should realize that it is not considered a commitment on his part, but rather a numerical guess based upon past experience. We are all aware of the discrepancies which often appear on estimates of time. These are usually self-protective. When estimates are padded, management must decide, if the task is completed early, whether or not to reward the individual for doing a good job although it probably could have been accomplished in less time.

Time estimates can be made in many kinds of units. The usual procedure is to use weeks and tenths-of-weeks using a five-day, forty hour week. However, some time estimates involve minutes, days, weeks, months, or other units.

When time estimates are made within the work flow, they are usually made on a random basis rather than a sequential or left to right basis in order to avoid a biasing effect. This procedure choses a task at random and secures estimates for it rather than beginning at the left and going completely to the right. This prevents individuals from adjusting their estimates for activities which come later in the project because of the estimates they made for tasks that come earlier. If we don't consider an adjustment made for sequential choice, project estimates of time frequently come out to a previously determined deadline date rather than an estimated date.

We earlier stated that for large projects of long duration it is not always necessary to detail the network in the subsequent periods. This is also true for securing time estimates in these projects. Detailed estimates of time, for the first year of a project, can be made with larger estimates of time for subsequent years of the project. Then, as we move through each succeeding phase, additional detail can be determined and incorporated into the network.

Regardless of the procedure or rules followed, we must recognize that the output data will be no better than the validity of the time estimates which are provided as input. Historical data and experience are invaluable aids for time estimates but, unfortunately, this data is not always available. Consequently, many estimates may be invalid and lead to a nonfunctional time base for the project. The project personnel must realize that the time estimation phase of project planning is extremely important.

Activity Time Estimation

The starting point for time estimation is the individual activity within the work plan. From the activity time estimates, other information that is useful to the project manager is calculated. This discussion, therefore, will focus upon activity time estimations before considering time calculations and their relationship to events and total project time.

When estimating the time for an activity, our first question is "How long will it take us to complete the task, given the nature of the task and an effective resource application rate?" In deterministic situations, a single estimate usually will provide the answer. Multiple time estimates are secured in the probabilistic situation. Here, the most common procedure is similar to procedure employed by the PERT technique. In the PERT technique, three estimates of time are usually given for each individual activity. These are identified as *optimistic*, *most likely*, and *pessimistic*. The optimistic time, usually symbolized by the small letter *a*, is based upon the assumption that everything will go well. This estimation proposes that an activity will have no more than one out of one hundred chances of being completed within this time. The most likely time, usually designated by the letter *m*, is the most realistic estimate of the time the activity may take. Usually it would be given when only a single estimate is requested. It reflects normal circumstances, and includes some success and some failure in carrying out the activity. The pessimistic estimate, usually designated by the small letter b, is the longest time an activity would take under the most adverse conditions. Like the optimistic time, it is assumed that this would occur only one time in one hundred. The pessimistic estimate reflects the possibility of failure, and the need to start all over again. This estimate must be carefully considered and chosen since it often is too optimistic and does not reflect the potential problems in the task. Whenever there is a reasonable doubt about performance specifications or the achievement of an activity goal, the pessimistic estimate should reflect this concern.

There has been a great deal of research and discussion about the validity of the PERT estimating technique. Some writers claim that the system underestimates project completion time, and, therefore, is invalid (12, 13). For our purposes, we will accept its basic assumptions, since the research on these assumptions is inconclusive at this time. It first assumes that the distribution of time estimates is not normal but rather, is similar to the one presented in Figure 7.1. This type of distribution is generally referred to as the *Beta distribution*. In actual practice, many estimates will not meet this basic assumption. Nevertheless, the developers felt that the theory of three time estimates and the Beta distribution was useful since their experience indicated that R and D tasks more often followed the pessimistic estimate than the optimistic estimate. R and D tasks are those tasks that are undertaken in research and development projects in which the outcome of the end product is uncertain. The development of new techniques, often from only paper ideas, offers unforseen problems and difficulties. These possible problems have to be considered in the planning effort. Hence, in time estimation one must also allow for them. This is done by providing an estimate for completion which accounts for the uncertain nature of the research and development activities. They realized that over- or undertime estimates might occur within the system. They felt, however, that these errors would be self-correcting during the project, since periodic estimates are obtained and, therefore, estimates are improved through increased experience or efficiency in making them. Another advantage sighted for this estimating procedure was the possibility that an estimator would be more willing to provide these ranges of times than a specific deterministic estimate.

Time estimates are gathered for all activities except the dummy activities discussed in Chapter 6. Since these tasks do not require any resources or effort, they are assigned time estimates of zero in either

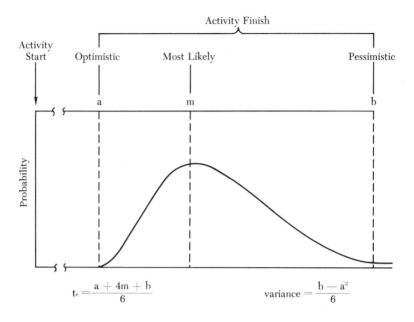

Figure 7.1

Activity Time Estimates Under Probabilistic Procedure.

the deterministic or probabilistic situation. There are some occasions, however, when we will need a period of time during which no work is going on or a period of waiting is involved, in order to arrive at a valid total time. In these cases, we employ a *real time* dummy activity. In this procedure, a time estimate is assigned to the dummy activity, which reflects the time involved in the dummy activity. For example, we might need to show the period of time between the ending of school in June and the beginning of school in September. No work may occur during this period so we would use a dummy activity, but the length of this period has to be considered. In working out the time estimation, a time would be assigned to the activity and would be included in any subsequent calculations.

Once the three individual time estimates are obtained, an *expected elapsed time* (t_e) is established for each activity. This is done by using the formula:

$$t_e = \frac{a + 4m + b}{6}$$

Once the t_e value is calculated, it can be placed on the network underneath the activity line. When the distance between the optimistic and the most likely estimate is equal to the distance between the most likely and pessimistic estimate, the expected elapsed time value will equal the most likely estimate. These types of estimates are referred to as *balanced estimates*. They may reflect the fact that the estimator has not given enough attention to the difficulties he may encountered in the activity and, therefore, should be questioned by the network specialist. The three estimates can also be used to measure the range of uncertainty existing within an activity. This range is referred to as *activity variance* and is calculated by the formula:

$$S^2_{t_e} = \left(\frac{6\text{-}a}{6} \right)^2$$

The variance estimate is used primarily for probability estimates about the meeting of a particular schedule date for an event. In the initial estimating phase, however, the variance estimate helps to identify those activities that may be potential trouble spots in the project. An activity with a large variance, for example, estimates of 2–10–30, indicates a job which requires careful surveillance. In contrast, an activity with estimates of 3–3–3 has no variance and probably is deterministic. Thus, the variance of an activity can become a useful piece of information for the manager and often is worth the time needed to calculate it. In some cases, activities with a large variance in the initial estimating phase are prime subjects for examination, and should be revised into smaller activities for a more realistic time estimation.

The variance concept was incorporated into the PERT system for the purpose of making probability statements about the accomplishment of events on schedule. This concept is not extensively used in many applications, so it is not discussed in detail here. Readers interested in the concept and its application should read the material presented in the Appendix.

Activity Start and Completion Times

The process of time estimating results in data generation for the information base, which will be used by management in planning and controlling the project. We need, now, to consider the times that events can take place. Most of the processes developed for showing the start and completion of activities involve assigning times to the events bounding the activity, rather than to the activity itself. To illustrate this procedure, let us employ the technique utilized in the probabilistic time estimation of the PERT method. This will generate information about the earliest time that an event can occur, the latest time it can occur and not delay another pathway in the project or the total project time, the critical path or most time consuming pathway through the network, and the amount of slack of free time associated with an activity, a pathway, or the total project.

The procedure for establishing the earliest event time (T_E) and the latest allowable event time (T_L) is essentially the same, except that they proceed through the network in different directions. Let us turn first to the calculations of the earliest event time. Figure 7.2 shows a simple network with an activity time placed on each of the activities. The calculation of the earliest expected event time, which is designated by the symbol (T_E) in order to distinguish it from the activity time estimate (t_e), is obtained by moving from left to right in the network, adding the activity time estimates along the various pathways. This process is exhibited in Figure 7.2, part B. In the normal procedure a T_E equal to 0 is assigned to the beginning event. However, at events 4 and 7 we have two activity arrows entering into the same event. In this case, we apply a rule of selecting the *largest* value going along both pathways. For example, the total time on pathway 1–2–4 equals seven weeks, while the total pathway time on 1–3–4 is only three weeks. Since we can not complete the work earlier than seven weeks along the top pathway, we assign a completion time of seven weeks. The same condition exists at event 7, except that now we must check the pathways 1–2–4–6–7, 1–3–4–6–7, and 1–3–5–7 in order to discover the longest pathway. The process involves moving from left to right, adding as we go, and applying the rule of selecting the largest value when two or more activities enter a particular event.

The process of calculating the latest allowable time, which is designated by the symbol T_L, is the reverse of the process for calculating the earliest event time. In this case, we start at the right of the network and move backwards or to the left subtracting as we go. Again, we employ a rule for two or more activities coming out of an event. This rule assigns the *smallest* value that we get in our calculation process, as illustrated in part C of Figure 7.2. Under normal circumstances we would have some type of date assigned for the final event of the project. In the planning situation, however, we often do not have a date available, since what we are trying to determine is the tentative completion time of the project. In this situation, we assign to the terminal event the same time we find going forward to begin our backward calculations. In Figure 7.2, part C, we assign event 7 the latest allowable time of 14 weeks. We then begin moving backwards in the network, subtracting the individual activity times from the times we get for the several events. The particular problem events

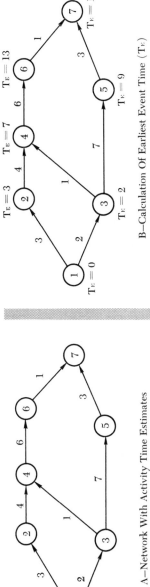

B—Calculation Of Earliest Event Time (T_E)

A—Network With Activity Time Estimates

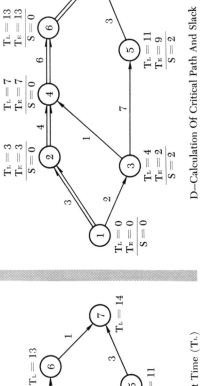

D—Calculation Of Critical Path And Slack

C—Calculation Of Latest Allowable Event Time (T_L)

Figure 7.2

Calculation Of Event Times.

in this case are numbers 3 and 1. To determine the latest allowable time for event 3, we substract the activity time of 7 from event 5 and get the latest allowable time for 4. We also subtract the activity time of 1 from event 4 and find a latest allowable time of 6. Here, we apply the rule of always selecting the smallest value. Hence, we would assign a T_L equal to 4 at event 3. An inspection of this network would show that it makes some sense. For example, event 3 would have to occur no later than four weeks if the pathway 3–5–7 is to be completed by 14 weeks. The same process is applied to event 1 in order to determine the latest allowable time for it.

Once we have generated the earliest expected event times and the latest allowable event times, two additional pieces of information can be generated for the project manager. The initial critical pathway, which is normally defined as the most time consuming pathway in the network, can be established. In our example, this will be the pathway 1–2–4–6–7. The critical path is identified with a unique symbol such as a double arrow line, colored line or some similar device. In addition to the critical path, the amount of free time or slack time associated with a particular event can be identified. We can identify it by subtracting the T_E values from the T_L values illustrated in part D of Figure 7.2.

One or two cautions should be made about both the critical path and the slack shown in the illustration. First, the zero slack condition existing on the critical path will be true only in those situations where the terminal event time obtained by going forward is used to initiate the backward calculations. In actual project operations, the critical path will probably vary from a negative slack condition to a positive slack condition. A negative slack will occur if the latest allowable date for project completion is less than the total expected completion time. A positive slack condition will exist when the total time for completion is greater than the estimated time for completion. Project managers should realize that there will be an initial Critical Path but as the project moves along and work becomes completed ahead or behind schedule, the overall critical path will change. Knowing exactly where the critical path is at any particular moment in the project is essential to successful management.

Second, the slack as shown in the illustration is normally associated with events. Hence, it is referred to as *Event Slack* The degree of slack, however, is associated with both the activities and events along a particular pathway. For example, the pathway 1–3–5–7 has a slack condition of two weeks available to it. The pathway running from 3–4 has a positive slack of four weeks associated with it. We do not have to reach event 4 until we are seven weeks into the project, but event 3 can occur as early as two weeks into the project. The job itself only takes one week which leaves a slack condition of four weeks. Knowing the amount of slack existing on a pathway or associated with an event or activity is a valuable piece of information for the project director.

In many discussions of network techniques, the reader will encounter the term *float*. Float is basically the same as slack, but it is sometimes referred to as *activity slack*, to distinguish it from event slack. The term *float* is used more extensively in the critical path method than in PERT. Both CPM and PERT, however, utilize the same basic concept. If one uses the CPM procedures, he will encounter expressions such as, *total float, free float early, free float late, independent float,* or *free float*. These terms are oriented toward the date when activities can be started and when they can be completed. Space does not permit a full discussion of these concepts, but Woodgate (21) has a good discussion of them.

The calculations described above are generally straight forward but some situations occur during which the calculation procedures will involve either the use of the no-time dummy activity, the real time dummy activity, or known scheduled dates for events or directed completion date for the project.

The calculation procedure used when the normal no-time and real time dummy activities appear in the network, is shown in Figure 7.3. In part A, there is a small network showing a no-time dummy. Part B of the same figure shows the real time dummy activity. We can see that there is a change in the earliest expected time, latest allowable time and slack for event 3 in these two cases.

The calculation procedure used when internal event schedule dates (T_S) are provided and or a known project completion date (T_D) has been assigned is illustrated in Figure 7.4. In part A, time calculations are shown for a small network where no scheduled or directed dates have been incorporated. Part B shows that a directed date of 20 weeks has been assigned to the terminal event and a scheduled date of 10 weeks has been given for event 8. Forward calculations are made as usual. When the backward calculations are made, a time of 20 weeks is assigned at event 10, and calculations are made until event 8 is reached. Furthermore, backward calculations are then made, using the time of 10 weeks rather than 13 weeks which might have been used if a time of 10 weeks had not been assigned. The assignment of this date creates a negative slack condition along the critical path up

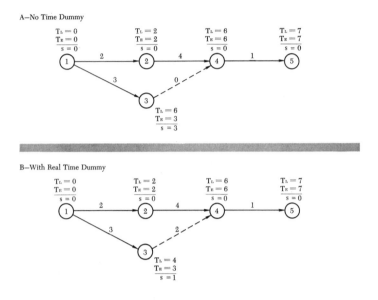

Figure 7.3

Time Calculation With No Time And Real Time Dummy Activity.

to event 10 but positive slack on the rest of the pathway. Adjustments will have to be made in the network to eliminate the negative slack condition.

Procedures for Network Time Adjustments

The previous procedures for establishing the start and completion times for individual events and activities as well as the total project time assumed that no particular directed or scheduled finished date had been assigned to the terminal event. When a terminal event date is known in advance, we would insert it at the final event. Our calcula-

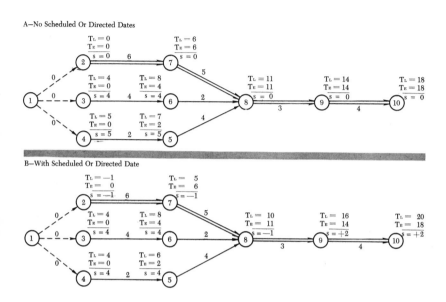

Figure 7.4

*Illustration Of Event Time Calculations With
Known Scheduled And Directed Dates.*

tions might simply show that the expected time for the project would
take longer than the total time available represented by the directed
completion date and the planned start date. In these cases, we must
adjust the network in order to meet the directed date. We must reduce
the total time by employing several procedures either singularly or in
combination.

Adding Resources. We could add additional resources to an activity, particularly an activity which is limiting or serving as a constraint.
This will allow us to be sure that the activity is accomplished on

time, or even possibly reduce the time needed for it. Our ability to use this procedure will depend upon the availability of resources, or our ability to manipulate and assign the resources as needed.

Activity Redefinition. We might also want to consider the possibility of redefining or changing a particular activity and, thereby, shorting the expected time for it. For example, a particular activity might consist of mailing 1,000 questionnaires, and the time estimate might be based upon accomplishing this task. The work could be reduced by mailing out only 500 questionnaires. This reduces the time estimate by a relative amount. We should note, however, that in exercising this option we have modified the performance level that we may have wanted to maintain. That is, the results from 500 questionnaires might not be as good as the results from 1,000 questionnaires.

Paralleling Activities. In most cases, the development of a work flow represents an "ideal" sequence of steps. It is highly desirable that certain steps preceed other steps to insure that the final product will be a quality item. In order to gain some time, however, we could reduce the linear work flow to one showing work going on concurrently or in parallel. In moving from a linear to a concurrent array, it must be remembered that the final product may not be as good since its successful completion is affected by moving to a less desirable work flow.

Eliminating Activities. Sometimes, certain activities which are not essential for the successful completion of the project can be eliminated. This option may seem somewhat contradictory because all our efforts have been focused upon including all work which has to be done. Many networks, however, have certain activities that can be eliminated, particularly those that serve as planned constraints and not real constraints. The elimination of these events will not jeopardize the successful completion of the project. Other alternatives are applied only after this one has been given careful consideration.

Modified Performance Requirements. It is also possible to reduce the total performance requirements of the project. That is, simply reduce the quality of the item that we produce. For example, a project dealing with a review of literature covering a fifty year period of time, and including most known journals, books, and publications relating to the field could reduce the years being covered, and the journals being included. When this type of adjustment is used, the performance requirements are changed.

SUMMARY

These procedures can be employed either singularly or in combination to make an adjustment in time. They are utilized not only in the planning stage but also in the actual operation to make adjustments for the problems that are presented during the course of the project. The processes result in what might be called a planned schedule but not a scheduled plan. The subject of the next chapter will be scheduling a plan.

One of the features of the PERT system which distinguished it from other management systems was the introduction of statistical concepts as a technical part of the planning and controlling functions. While the statistical aspects have not been widely employed, an understanding of their purpose and nature should be secured by any one intending to use the particular technique. Due to its limited use in actual practice and the many questions which have been raised about its basic assumptions, no extended discussion of the statistical probability aspects of time estimation has been presented in the chapter. A brief discussion of the procedures has been included as an Appendix to this book. The basic processes are not difficult to grasp if one understands the normal deviate "z" as used in the normal curve probability tables.

Check List for Time Estimation Phase

Listed below are several questions which can be used as a guide or a check list for ensuring that the necessary actions have been taken in developing time estimates, before entering into the scheduling or resource allocation phase described in the next chapter.

1. Have time estimates, either deterministic or probabilistic, been secured for each of the activities or work tasks?

2. Are directed dates or project completion dates known and available?

3. Have any required internal schedule dates been established?

4. Have the various time calculations both for events and activities been double checked for accuracy?

5. If a computer has been used to process initial time calculations, have the input forms been checked for completeness and accuracy before key punching?

6. Has an analysis been made of either manual calculations or computer outputs to note slack conditions or probability associated with events?

7. Have the reasonableness of the problems identified by an analysis of calculations been verified by the use of cross checks to locate errors in calculations, input data, or processing?

8. Have the critical and other pathways been analyzed to determine the nature of constraints?

9. Have potential problem areas (limited slack, questionable activities), been discussed with responsible units or personnel for proposed solutions?

10. Have solutions for potential problems been identified, initial calculations revised, and new time data information generated?

11. Have the final work flow plans with time estimates developed, been approved by appropriate and necessary levels of management?

References

1. Bailey, G. C., *Predicting Research and Development Performance Time*. Bethesda, Maryland: International Business Machines Corporation, Federal Systems Division, 1962.
2. Bailey, G. C., *Research and Development Performance Time Estimation*. Bethesda, Maryland: Management Science Report MS-2, International Business Machines Corporation, 1962.
3. Clark, Charles E., "The PERT Model for the Distribution of an Activity Time," *Operations Research*, X, No. 3 (June, 1962), pp. 405-07.
4. Cook, Desmond L., *PERT: Applications in Education*. Cooperative Research Monograph Number 17, U. S. Office of Education, 1966, Chapter 2.
5. Donaldson, W. A., "The Estimation of the Mean and Variance of a PERT Activity Time," *Operations Research*, XIII, No. 3 (June, 1965), pp. 382-85.
6. Grubbs, Frank E., "Attempts to Validate Certain PERT Statistics," or "Picking on PERT," *Operations Research*, Vol. X (1962), pp. 912-16.
7. Ferguson, John D., "Determining the Probability of Meeting a Schedule with PERT," *Journal of Data Management*, Vol. III (June 1965), p. 89.
8. Hill, L. S., *Towards an Improved Basis of Estimation and Controlling R and D Tasks*. Santa Monica, California: RAND Corporation, (May) 1966.

9. King, W. R., "Project Planning Using Network Simulation," *Pittsburg Business Review,* Vol. IX (September 1968), pp. 1-8.

10. King, W. R. and T. A. Wilson, "Subjective Time Estimates in Critical Path Planning—A Preliminary Analysis", *Management Sciences* XIII, No. 5 (January 1967), pp. 307-20.

11. King, W. R., and D. M. Wittevronel, and K. D. Hezel, "On the Analysis of Critical Path Time Estimating Behavior," *Management Sciences,* Vol. XIV (September 1967), pp. 79-84.

12. Lukaszewicz, Josef, "On the Estimation of Errors Introduced by Standard Assumption Concerning the Distribution of Activity Duration in PERT Calculations," *Operations Research,* XIII, No. 3 (March, 1965).

13. MacCrimmon K. R. and C. A. Ryavec, *An Analystic Study of the PERT Assumptions.* Santa Monica, California: The RAND Corporation, 1962. (See also *Operations Research* XII, No. 5 (Jan., 1964), pp. 16-37.)

14. Malcolm, D. G., J. H. Roseboom, C. E. Clark, and W. Fazar, "Application of a Technique for Research and Development Program Evaluation," *Operations Research,* VII, No. 5 (September 1959), pp. 646-69.

15. Murray, John E., "Consideration of PERT Assumptions," *IEEE Transactions on Engineering Management,* EM-10 (September 1963).

16. *PERT Fundamentals,* "Vol. 1—Networking", Washington, D.C.: U.S. Government Printing Office.

17. *PERT Program Evaluation Research Task.* Summary Report, Phase 1, Special Projects Office, Washington, D.C.: Bureau of Naval Weapons, Department of the Navy, (July) 1958.

18. *A Procedure for Estimating Cost, Time, and Reliability in Development Training.* Vienna, Virginia: Bird Engineering-Research Associates, Inc., 1963.

19. Stackfleth, E. D., *The Reliability and Validity of Various Techniques of Estimating Task Times,* Unpublished Doctoral Dissertation, Purdue University, 1965.

20. Welsh, D. J. A., "Errors Introduced by A PERT Assumption," *Operations Research,* XIII, No. 1 (Jan., 1965), pp. 141-43.

21. Woodgate, H. S., *Planning by Network.* London, England: Business Publications Limited, 1964, Chapters 5 and 6.

chapter **8**

Scheduling and Resource Allocation

The previous steps in the planning process have focused upon defining the objectives of the project, identifying the major work elements, establishing a work flow for the various efforts, and securing time estimates for each task in the work flow as well as the total estimated time. The next step is the establishment of schedules and allocation of resources to work efforts.

During the prior planning activities, schedules were not considered in order to prevent biases in the estimates of the activity time durations as well as the total project completion time. It is not unusual for a project director to establish for himself some scheduled completion date. Yet, the scheduled completion date for the project will be established through the activities of the planning phase. When the scheduled completion date is known in advance, the activity time estimations often too conveniently fit the scheduled completion date. When this type of time adjustment occurs, the value of management systems is diminished. In developing or establishing schedules for a project, some adjustment usually has to be made in the activity time estimations. These changes or modifications are not done in a haphazard manner simply to comply with a scheduled completion date.

Project scheduling is not easy and has many associated problems. The scheduling process has been the subject of a great deal of research and general approaches, models, and algorithms have been developed. Discussions of the scheduling problem by Clark (1), Wiest (10), Woodgate (12), Davis (4), and Rosenbloom (9) present ideas about scheduling problems which the reader may want to examine for further information. This chapter will discuss the general dimensions of scheduling as well as the major problems or situations confronting the project manager in developing a schedule.

Scheduling Defined

Scheduling is defined in this chapter as the translation of the developed plan into a time table, showing the calendar date for the start and completion of work. The scheduled start and end of each activity or work package as well as the total project is emphasized. The schedule helps to determine the operating budget for the project and permits us to allocate resources to the activities.

It is within the scheduling process that we become concerned with competition for one or more of the resources that may exist in an organization. In establishing a schedule for the project, we are concerned not only with the time to do a job but also with the exact date that the office involved may be able to do our work, having considered all the other projects in the organization that will utilize this same resource. The planned schedule, which is generated as an output of the scheduling process, enables the project director to judge event progress and forecast a date of completion. The scheduling process also enables the project director to inform various organizational units of the schedules that they must maintain for their particular task.

The concept of *resource allocation* is closely associated with the concept of scheduling. Once the work flow or plan is accepted, it is translated into a schedule by the assignment of resources which will accomplish the planned activities. If it could be assumed that unlimited resources would be available, then the time estimates obtained earlier could be automatically translated into a schedule. In most practical situations, however, only limited resources are available to the project manager. Consequently, a schedule must be developed by allocating these resources in the best possible way. Resource requirements and needs are determined in both the initial planning stages and the necessary replanning stages during the project operation phase. Establishing the needed resource requirements for each activity and the total project is a necessary prerequisite for budget preparation. Resource requirements and schedules determine how many and for how long a resource is needed. These needs are reflected in the budget. Resource allocation, as it is used here, generally refers to personnel needs. Nevertheless, under this concept it is possible to include materials, supplies, facilities, travel, and other items required to complete a task or total project.

Some Scheduling Constraints

On the surface, the process of scheduling appears relatively simple. Several constraints, however, make the process somewhat difficult and often lead to the development of less than an ideal or optimum schedule. Some constraints are given in the following list (8).

1. The availability of particular resources during specific calendar periods.
2. The general sequence of the work in the project plan.
3. Consideration of resource requirements of other present or future projects.
4. Different or conflicting demands on the same resource.
5. A desire to avoid peak load for particular skills.
6. The available local capacity to do a particular task.
7. Limitations and requirements imposed by funding agencies.
8. Desire to minimize overtime and idle time.
9. Necessary integration with other plans or projects using the same resources.
10. The manager's judgment of a reasonable time for performing activities of an uncertain nature.
11. Technical constraints such as uncertainties which may require extra time.
12. Local personnel policies concerning work practices (vacations, sick leave, etc.).
13. National, state, and local laws governing work practices.
14. Difficulties inherent in scheduling far in advance.
15. The varying number of work days in a month and their translation into calendar dates.

Many of these constraints relate to project scheduling in the business-military complex, but have some application to the educational situation. The educational situation, in contrast, has some unique constraints which can affect schedules. Notable among these is the nine to ten month period in which educational personnel operate. Schedules conform to this time period largely because of resource availability. Furthermore, needed resources cannot always be as easily obtained or terminated as they can in other sectors of the economy. Short term employment of professional personnel except on a consulting or leave basis, is also rare in the field of education. Studies should be made about the other special considerations in the education and their affect on the scheduling process.

Obviously, there are many factors or constraints which can result in the establishment of schedules that project manager considers less than desirable.

What is a Good Schedule?

We have already noted the desire to create an ideal or optimum schedule. Unfortunately, an ideal or optimum schedule rarely can be generated in a practical situation. Instead, the project manager must generate a "reasonable" schedule. In doing so, he must form the criterion of reasonableness. Some possible criteria are: (1) to complete the project in a minimum amount of time; (2) to complete the project with a minimum amount of cost; (3) to maximize performance in the project. A further criterion might be to "level" the utilization of resources over a period of time. A schedule that is developed for only one of these criteria probably will not meet the needs of the criteria. For example, the recent Apollo Program presented a schedule which maximized the performance of the systems rather than the completion of the program in the least possible time. The performance emphasis was evidenced by the decision to continue the Apollo IX and X flights rather than skipping them after the successful flight of Apollo VIII.

The most typical criterion is the one associated with the least cost. That is, schedules are generated to minimize the costs that are associated with the resources used in the project. Instead of thinking of an ideal or optimum schedule, perhaps Wiest's suggestion should be followed (10). He refers to a feasible schedule which enables him to observe the job and/or task sequence and times, avoiding the violation of necessary resource constraints and maintaining the scheduled project completion time.

Developing the Initial Schedule

The sequence of steps involved in scheduling a project have not been as well formulated as they have been for other dimensions of project planning. There appears to be no sequence of operations that enables the project manager to "automatically" generate a schedule. Given the unusual situation of completely unlimited resource availability, the expected times that are established for each activity in the estimating phase should automatically generate the schedule. It should be fairly easy to translate the T_E and T_L dates into a schedule since the effective flow of resources will carry them on. Usually, however, the resources are limited, and some adjustment must be made in order to develop a realistic schedule. These adjustments may cause a change in the configuration of the network in order to produce the project within available resources. The planned sequence of work, however, is not changed unless it is absolutely necessary.

Decentralized vs. Centralized Schedules

The actual steps in scheduling can follow almost the same rule of moving from specific to general or general to specific observed in the work flow and time estimations. These two approaches are often referred to as the *centralized* and *decentralized* approach. In the centralized approach, high levels of management establish project schedules for milestone events. Lower levels are requested to conform to the scheduled dates. Decentralized scheduling involves the establishment of schedules at lower levels of management and the development of the overall project schedule from these schedules. Each procedure present unique problems. In the centralized scheduling approach, lower level scheduling may be difficult because job requirements, resource limitations and similar factors are not known. In the decentralized scheduling approach, more slack for setting necessary start dates within the work flow requirements is usually required. The solution is a compromise. Rough general schedules are set at the central level, and detailed schedules are established at the operating levels.

Scheduling Steps

Without emphasizing either the centralized or decentralized approach, establishing a schedule begins with the individual activities and work packages. Giving consideration to the resource availability, a scheduled elapsed time maybe shorter or longer than the estimated time for the activity. A scheduled end date can be determined for the terminal event, if a scheduled start date has been provided. Forward and backward time calculations can be used to establish the earliest schedule completion dates and the latest schedule completion dates for each event, as we did in the time estimating phase.

If, upon completion of this step, the total time exceeds the time available or the total costs are exceeded, readjustments will have to be made, using the procedures of paralleling activities, eliminating tasks, redefining work scope, and adjusting resources. The adjustment continues until a schedule is devised that meets the criterion established by the manager.

In developing the schedule, the manager should realize the slack existing on the pathways in the work flow. If the manager is aware of how much and where slack exists, activities on noncritical paths can be moved until resources are available; their duration can be extended in order to reduce resource utilization during a given period of time, or even possibly split into segments for different scheduled periods. Splitting into segments can only be done when it is possible to complete the task in segments. The activities on the critical path are not changed unless it is absolutely necessary.

This process of scheduling can be represented by a bar chart or schedule graph. Visual representation of the project work flow and associated free time allows the project manager to rearrange a given task in order to develop a satisfactory schedule. Figures 8.1 and 8.2 show a simplified illustration of a scheduling procedure which has as its criterion a more level flow of tasks than originally existed. It is still, however, constrained to the same finish date.

In Figure 8.1, the critical path has been identified by the solid black set, while activities and pathways not on the critical path have been identified by plain white boxes. Inspection of the figure reveals that in the present schedule, there are a number of tasks to be accomplished during the initial period of the project. A study of this chart reveals that there is some free time which can be utilized to match resource availability. The project manager, wishing to maintain a more even work flow, has adjusted the scheduled start and end dates of various tasks as shown in Figure 8.2. He has taken advantage of the slack conditions, and yet the completion date of the project as well as the internal dates for activities has not been violated. The manager could have adjusted the schedule by starting all the activities as late as possible. In this case, tasks would have piled up towards the end of the project rather than at its beginning.

There is no specific criterion for the manager to employ in this situation. He must use his own knowledge and experience. Perhaps it is unwise for the manager to generate a schedule which places the start and completion of activities towards the end of the project since any problems will further delay the projected scheduled end. The proper use of the free time represented by the slack condition can

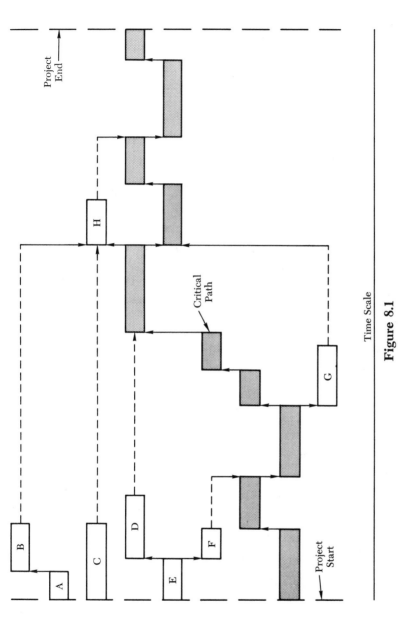

Figure 8.1

Illustration Of Schedule Development By Bar Chart I.

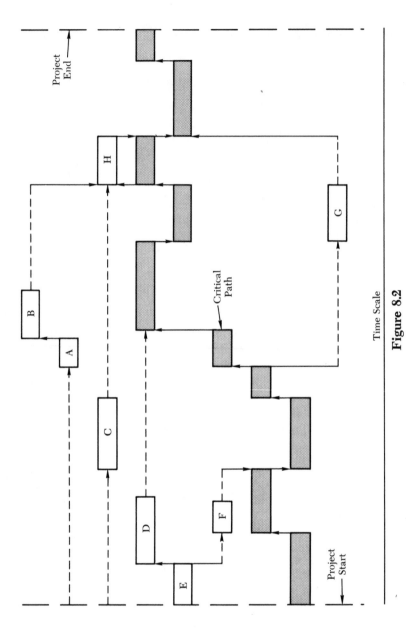

Figure 8.2

Illustration Of Schedule Development By Bar Chart II.

132

lead to a feasible schedule. Using the bar chart procedure, charts can be prepared for a centralized schedule at the top level of management, while individual units can make similar charts for their own use. Some business supply houses and management consulting firms have developed slotted boards, tab and string procedures, and similar graphic devices that help to portray schedules and resource requirements.

The development of an initial schedule is a repetitious process. If a computer is used to process much of the work flow data, then several different trial schedules can be established before deciding upon the working schedule for the project. The effect of adding resources, paralleling activities and other management actions can be studied first. These simulations can be made without a computer. Adjustments in the schedule during the course of the project are common. Time, however, is important in making the readjustment. Hand calculations present difficulties which are usually overcome by the use of a computer.

RESCHEDULING

Once the project is initiated and operations are begun, the project will need to be rescheduled from time to time. The project manager should not assume that the initial schedule will be maintained throughout the life of the project. This condition would be desirable but schedules can be disrupted for many reasons. A change in the major or supporting objective of a project may lead to a rescheduling of the project internally. For example, in conducting the PERT project under a grant from the Office of Education, the final report was to have the traditional format. During the course of the project, the author was advised that the funding agency wanted a manuscript that could be published and distributed in place of the report. This change required some rescheduling of the internal operations within the project. Another factor that may cause rescheduling might be a change in the work flow necessary to achieve an objective. The schedule may have to be changed because of certain slippages which have occurred because of unusual delays in completing an activity, or because of increases in slack time due to the early completion of an activity. Another cause of rescheduling may be a change in funding. The funding may go higher or lower. In either case, a different schedule may have to be generated.

PROBLEMS IN SCHEDULING

There are many different problems associated with the scheduling process. Several general problems appear to give the most concern to project directors. These four problems have been the object of research and study. Each of them will now be discussed briefly.

The Fixed Duration Time Problem

This scheduling problem arises when there is a constraint upon the total project duration time. That is, there is a fixed time by which the project must be completed. This situation usually arises, as Woodgate (12) and others have pointed out, when the project manager has produced sufficient resources to carry out the project but wishes to carry them at a constant rate, making the most effective use of them. This concept is often referred to as "manpower leveling". A simplified example of the manpower leveling concept is presented in Figure 8.3. In this brief example, a study has been made of the times at which a resource skill, a statistician in this case, will be needed. This type of graph is sometimes referred to as a resource profile. Figure 8.3 shows that the rate of application is uneven. By adjusting the activities within the stated duration time, a more even rate of application can be found. Similar charts can be prepared for the other resources in the project. The solution is similar to that illustrated by the bar chart. Visual inspection is made of the work, and the flow of activities is adjusted to even out the resource application.

The Fixed Resources Problem

This scheduling problem arises when a project manager has a pool of resources which cannot be exceeded. His objective is to schedule the activities in a way that minimizes any possible increase in the total project time. He should realize that, because of the limitations on resources, the project will have to be extended by some small amount, but this increase must be kept to a minimum.

The solution to this problem lies in the following steps. Activities on noncritical pathways throughout the project are delayed until the manpower needed for them is available. Activities on the various slack pathways or noncritical paths are also lengthened. Instead of taking one week to do the job, perhaps two weeks are scheduled with the resource in effect for half of that activity. If the resource requirement is still excessive after these two procedures have been employed,

A—Resource Profile For A Statistician Before Schedule Adjustment

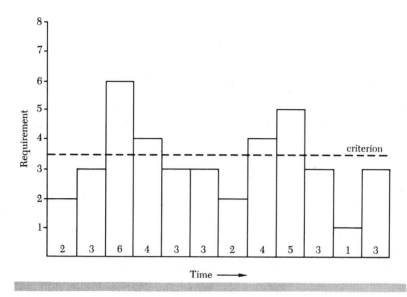

B—Resource Profile For A Statistician After Schedule Adjustment

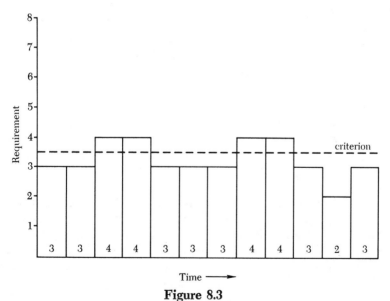

Figure 8.3

Illustration Of Manpower Leveling Concept.

the critical path should be examined to determine the greatest reduction in resource requirements per unit of time increase in the project duration. Some activities can have the resource requirements reduced but in reducing them, the activity will be considerably extended. Other activities can have a resource requirement reduced and not result in as large an increase in time. Given a choice, the resource requirement for an activity would be reduced that would least increase the time. The project manager must recognize the effect that changes in the critical path activities—either their delay or extension—will have on the other slack pathways. This process continues until the resource requirements have been reached.

Weist (10) has discussed a unique dimension of the limited resources situation. He states that, in this particular situation, the critical path in the sense of time may lose its meaning. It may be more useful, he feels to think of a critical *sequence* which is determined by the technological sequence and/or resource sequence associated with jobs. There may be a certain sequence of tasks in the project that depend first of all upon the successful technological advances or upon the availability of resources. These sequences may be more meaningful and useful to the project director than the time sequence represented by the critical path. Schedules may have to be developed on this basis.

The Time/Cost Trade Off Concept Problem

Scheduling can become a major problem if either time or resources are constrained to certain limits. Some of the specific scheduling models such as PERT and CPM do not take into account limited resources. Therefore, they are not as useful as scheduling techniques. If there are no constraints on either resources or time, the problem becomes a time/cost trade off. This concept has limited value in educational research and development situations. Its greatest application has been made in the construction industry and other trades where there is enough data accumulated about the time and cost associated with a particular job.

The concept assumes that for any given activity or total project a time/cost relationship or a time/cost curve can be established. It further assumes that this curve is convex as shown in Figure 8.4. In practice, we do not know the true activity cost curve, but if we can identify a "normal" time and a "crash" time, two points are available which can be plotted as illustrated in Figure 8.4. These two points can be connected then and a linear approximation to the true curve can be developed. If enough data were available, we could plot a relationship

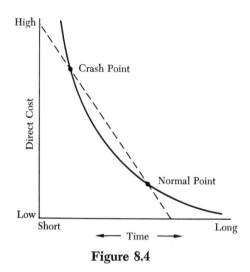

Figure 8.4

Illustration Of True Time/Cost Relationship For Project Activity.

between time and cost for each activity in the work plan. The slope of the line probably would be different for each activity. Reductions in time for one task might be accompanied by increases in cost while a reduction in time in another activity might be accompanied by a slight increase in cost. Under this concept, a time reduction is made in the activity which will result in giving the least cost to the total project. A few computer programs analyze a network in this fashion, if the necessary data has been established as input. It then adjusts the total project schedule accordingly. This procedure essentially optimizes costs by generating what might be called a *least cost schedule*.

Multi-Project Scheduling Problem

We have been discussing scheduling as it relates to a single project directed by one project manager. In many organizations, several projects go on simultaneously under different project managers. These projects draw upon several common resources of the organization. Consequently conflicts arise about the utilization of the resources. The employment of the previous procedures makes the work flow for a particular department more even and insures that the work of the projects will be accomplished according to the schedule. The reader interested in learning more about these multi-project scheduling techniques may want to investigate the Resource-Allocation in Multi-

Project Situation (RAMPS) developed by CEIR, Inc. (5), and the PROMIS system developed by Burroughs Corporation (13), as well as the chapter on multi-project scheduling on Woodgate's book on network planning (12).

SUMMARY

Most of the above procedures tend to operate under a set of heuristic rules developed as much from experience as any theory of scheduling. A principal concern in the project situation, particularly in R and D tasks, is the uncertainty problem. As educational personnel gain experience and knowledge in R and D activities, scheduling problems should be reduced. This chapter outlined the general process used in developing schedules and determining the time and place at which various resources will be needed. Once the schedule has been established and resource requirements carefully determined to meet the schedule, the project manager is ready to prepare an estimate of cost to complete the project. Chapter 9 will describe the general processes of cost estimation and budget preparation.

Check List for Project Scheduling and Resource Allocation

The following are several questions which should be asked during the process of preparing the schedule and allocating resources to the project. They will help to establish a workable schedule for the project.

1. Has a criterion (or criteria) been established to serve as a guide for the scheduling process?

2. Have any directed dates or known scheduled dates been obtained and inserted into the scheduling discussions?

3. Have scheduling constraints such as legal holidays, vacation periods and related factors been considered?

4. Have efforts been made to determine the availability of specialized resources (consultants, equipment, etc.) and their impact on the schedule?

5. Is the scheduling process operating under a basic time constraint or a basic resource constraint condition?

6. Have needed adjustments in work tasks (breaking-up, stretching-out, movement on slack path), been made before any adjustments are made on the critical path?

7. Have scheduled dates been clearly established and associated with control points (milestone events, etc), in the project?

8. Has the initial schedule been reviewed and approved by management?

9. Has the schedule been disseminated to work units and staff offices?

References

1. Clark, C. E., "The Optimum Allocation of Resources Among the Activities of a Network," *Journal of Industrial Engineering*, Vol. XII (January 1961), pp. 11-17.
2. Clarke, R. W., "Activity Costing—Key to Progress in Critical Path Analysis," *IRE Transactions on Engineering Management*, EM-7 (March 1962), pp. 132-36.
3. Cook, D. L., *PERT: Applications in Education*. USOE Cooperative Research Monograph Number 17, Washington, D.C.: U.S. Office of Education, 1966.
4. Davis, E. W., "Resource Allocation in Project Network Models—A Survey," *Journal of Industrial Engineering*, Vol. XVII (April 1966), pp. 177-88.
5. Lambourn, S., "Resource Allocation and Multi-project Scheduling—A New Tool in Planning and Control," *The Computer Journal*, Vol. V (January 1963), pp. 300-04.
6. Moder, J. T., and C. R. Phillips, *Project Management with PERT and CPM*. New York: Reinhold Publishing Company, 1964. Chapters 5 and 6.
7. *PERT Fundamentals*, "Vol. II—Scheduling and Planning," Washington, D.C.: PERT Orientation and Training Center.
8. *PERT . . . Guide to Management Use*, PERT Coordinating Group, Office of the Secretary of Defense, Washington, D.C., 1963.
9. Rosenbloom, R. S., "Notes on the Development of Network Models for Resource Allocation in R and D Projects," *IRE Transactions on Engineering Management*, EM-11 (June 1964), pp. 58-63.

10. Wiest, J. D., *The Scheduling of Large Projects with Limited Resources.* Office of Naval Research, Memo #113, Graduate School of Industrial Administration, Carnegie Institute of Technology, Pittsburgh, Pennsylvania, 1962.
11. Woodgate, H. S., *Planning by Network.* London, England: Business Publications Ltd., 1964.
12. _____, "Planning Networks and Resource Allocation," *Datamation,* Vol. XIV (January 1968), pp. 36-43.
13. PROMIS Time Module, Reference Manual, Detroit, Michigan: Burroughs Corporation (June), 1968.

chapter **9**

Cost Estimation and Budget Preparation

The implementation of any planning effort, particularly a project, will require a certain amount of money in order to accomplish the projected work. These funds pay for personnel, equipment, travel, and related items. The success of the project will depend largely upon the funds that are available. The project manager must find a procedure that will help him to develop a realistic estimate of the needed funds. Under funding an operation can embarrass a manager as much as over funding. Either situation is a case of management inefficiency.

This chapter will outline the problems and procedures involved in securing cost estimates and their subsequent compiling into a *budget*. Budgets usually are prepared as a last step in the planning phase. Unfortunately, in many cases there is little relation between the proposed work and schedule, and the amount of funds needed for the project.

Before discussing some procedures that may be used in preparing a project budget, a review of elementary budgeting concepts is needed, since many people in the field of education have had no prior experience with budgeting or contracting.

ELEMENTARY BUDGET CONCEPTS

A budget is the expression, in financial terms, of a management plan for operating and financing a project during a specific time period. It is a predetermined detailed plan of action developed and distributed as a guide to current operations, and used as a partial standard for evaluating performance.

This definition emphasizes the planning and controlling functions of a budget. As a planning device, it simply transfers actions to dollars. Both the complexity of the process and the amount of detail in the budget will vary considerably from one organization to another and from one project to another. The degree of detail depends upon the person preparing the budget, but it should contain enough detail to be used as a control device. As controlling mechanisms, budgets are used in three ways: (1) as a means of organizing and directing a large segment of the management process; (2) as a means of guiding day-to-day management decisions; and (3) as a mark against which to measure actual performance.

The budgeting process forces managers to make a critical examination of the objectives, functions, methods, and costs of project. This process forces managers to *quantify* their plans and, therefore, facilitates the comparison of various plans on a cost-benefit basis. It also draws many people into the management process by requiring their participation in its construction.

A budget has certain limitations which must be recognized. Regardless of the review process for correcting budgeting errors, any plan that projects into the future will contain a certain degree of inaccuracy. A review process may reduce these inaccuracies, but it probably cannot eliminate them. A budget may also impart some inflexibility to operations in at least two ways. A project may be close to completion but in need of additional funds. If they are not available, project performance standards may have to be lowered. Sometimes, the concept of "earmarked" funds may limit a budget. One segment of a project may need additional funds while another segment may be below budget, but due to the project contract or the accounting system, the funds from one area cannot be transferred to the other area. This type of funding appears to be excessively restrictive. If widespread fund shifts were allow, there would be no reason to require a budget broken into various categories and sub-plans. Inaccuracies may be forced into a budget by the policies of the funding organization. Furthermore, budgeting is a once-a-year process that covers the coming year. The fact that it may be difficult to anticipate the needs for the entire year is probably a major cause for "padding" budgets. Projects funded through the U.S. Office of Education are often longer than a year, and, in many cases, a final budget must be submitted with the proposal, making reasonable estimates difficult.

Finally, budgets must be operable. That is, a budget is more than a paper exercise. It will lose much of its value if individuals do not use it as a guide to their actions. This in itself has some negative connotations by subduing individual freedom of action to a piece of paper.

Common Budget Terms

Before proceeding to a description of methods of budget preparation, there are a few terms with which the reader should be familiar.

Direct Costs.   Direct costs are the costs that can be directly traced to or associated with a particular activity or task of a project. There is no specific relationship between a direct cost input and the product of a project. For example, the product of a project may be a report containing recommendations for a teacher training curriculum. If a videotape machine had to be purchased for this project, then the machine is a direct cost but not a part of the final product.

Indirect Costs.   Indirect costs are costs that cannot be traced to a particular activity, task, or costing unit. There are two ways of distinguishing indirect costs from direct costs. Either they are incurred jointly by more than one activity, or they are individually too small to be economically assigned to any one costing unit. Electricity and heating charges are examples of a joint cost while thumbtacks and paperclips are examples of costs to small to be assigned to one costing unit. Indirect costs are frequently referred to as *overhead.*

Fixed Costs.   Some costs must be incurred in order to provide the supplies for an activity. These costs are incurred only once. The videotape machine referred to in direct costs would be a *fixed* cost. It is paid for once, and its cost has nothing to do with how much it is used. A certain portion of the electricity charge is fixed since there will always be some electrical consumption. While this charge occurs more than once, the fact that a certain amount will be charged each month qualifies it as a fixed cost. From these examples, it should be evident that fixed costs can be either direct (videotape machine), or indirect (electricity).

Variable Costs.   Variable costs are the costs, which when totaled, depend on the level of activity during the period. For example, the cost of materials for the videotape machine will vary with the machine usage. A portion of the electricity charges will be fixed, but the other portion will depend, for example, on the amount of night work. Variable costs also can be either direct or indirect.

Costing Unit.   A costing unit, also referred to as a *cost center*, refers to a work package or a segment of a work package for which the costs of operation are accumulated. It is possible for a single activity to be designated as a cost unit, but this is not ordinarily done unless the activity is critically important and commands a significant portion of the project funds. The types of cost units depend on how the costs were estimated. If the costs for certain activities were estimated, then the activities might be designated logically as cost units. Usually, however, costs are estimated by work packages which in turn become cost units. However the information derived from a cost unit should be worth more than the accounting costs incurred to find it.

Funding Arrangements

The project manager may or may not have a choice in the funding arrangement. He should, however, have some knowledge of the types of funding arrangements he is likely to encounter. We will describe briefly some of the major types of funding arrangements which may be found in governmental and private funding agencies.

Grants.   The grant is the simplest arrangement for the support of a project. A grant is usually given for the advancement of knowledge, while a contract requires a specific product or output. Grants are similar to gifts, while contracts require services.

Fixed Price Type Contract.   This type of contract supports research and development when the desired objective and cost can be established prior to performance. It provides for the performance of specified research usually within a specified time and cost. It is easy to administer, requires less detailed record keeping and auditing, and offers a great deal of flexibility for the internal adjustment of budget categories.

Cost Contract.   Under this arrangement, all allowable costs involved in performing a specific research project are paid. Normally, a total cost estimate for the project is required, and a maximum level of cost which cannot be exceeded, is established. If the organization exceeds its budget, it must do so at its own expense, or apply for further funds.

Cost-Sharing Contract. Under this arrangement both the funding and contracting organizations share in the cost of the project. The organizational share is often referred to as an "institutional allowance" or "contribution."

Cost Plus a Fixed Fee Contract. This contract is similar to the cost contract but provides for the payment of a fixed fee beyond what is allowed for cost reimbursement. USOE is beginning to award contracts to private profit-making non-educational institutions. As this practice grows, more of these contracts will probably be awarded.

With these elementary concepts of budgeting as a background, the succeeding sections of this chapter will present a comparison between traditional and emerging patterns of cost estimation and budget preparation.

TRADITIONAL BUDGETING METHOD

The traditional approach to a budget formulation is based upon the plans which have been developed. The breakdown of the budget begins and ends with a tabulation of requirements in categories such as personnel, materials and equipment, travel expenses, overhead, and miscellaneous expenses. A typical budget format is presented in Figure 9.1. Personnel is usually subdivided according to professional staff and clerical requirements. Materials and equipment are classified as either consumable supplies or permanent items such as texts and audio-visual equipment or large items such as computers and reproduction equipment. There may also be a special category for the rental of these items when they cannot be purchased. Sometimes, there is also a category called *institutional allowance* or *in-house funding*, which is frequently computed as the percentage of support which will be given to a project. This type of categorical budget is referred to as an *inputs* budget since it reflects the amount associated with the materials (inputs), needed to carry out the project operations.

The traditional budgeting procedure was not designed for the project situation, and, therefore, its methods are not carefully explicated. It is usually designed for the continuous operation situation in which next year's budget is derived from this year's expenditures allowing

South West Institute
for
New Developments and Leadership in Education
1000 Ermac Avenue
Cook City, Piedmont
00006
BUDGET SUMMARY

1. Project Title: _____   3. Total Time: _____

2. Funding Agency: _____   4. Dates:
                                                 From _____ To _____

Category	Funding Agency Contribution	SWINDLE Contribution
1. Personnel		
a. Salaries and wages		
b. Employee Benefits		
c. Indirect costs at 42%		
2. Materials and Supplies		
a. Project Materials		
b. Office Supplies		
3. Services		
4. Travel		
5. Communication		
6. Other Direct Costs	_____	
Subtotal, Direct Costs		
7. Agency Allowed Indirect Costs (Overhead)	_____	
TOTAL COSTS	_____	

Figure 9.1
Typical Traditional Budget Format.

for the possible expansion of services, salary increases, inflation, and other contingencies. Lower level cost centers determine the funds they will need for each category and submit their request to the next higher level which trims, eliminates, adjusts, and consolidates it before passing it up the organizational ladder. The preparation of these budgets is based on past experience. This procedure works since many organizations have large amounts of data concerning past or standard costs. The cost of new items may be difficult to determine, and these estimates are based on known related costs tempered by known future requirements and an additional percentage added as a safety factor.

This method presents many difficulties when it is applied to project budgeting since projects are not continuous operations. There is usually no past experience to draw upon. The project budget will be established and often cannot be added to once the contractual arrangement is established. The preparation of a realistic budget becomes, therefore, a serious problem. The duration of a project may not be great, but defining project output and the steps used to produce the output make budgeting and extremely difficult and complicated process.

The procedures for preparing budgets for a project usually are designed by an individual or a group and reviewed by some higher authority. The project manager attempts to determine the types of personnel needed and the period of time for which they will be needed, as well as the types of travel and supplies. The realism of the final budget prepared under these methods is doubtful. Statements such as "it appears that we need a full time project director" or "we will need to buy some computer time" are eventually carried into the budget without rational or logical justification. Sometimes the budget seems to have been prepared by one group and the project proposal by another group. Under these conditions, it often is difficult to relate resource needs to the work to be performed in any meaningful way.

The traditional type of budget prepared for project planning and control is more restrictive than the type described above. It functions as an accounting budget rather than a management budget. The expenditures made during the course of the project are charged against several categories. A monthly statement showing how much money has been spent in a budget category, what commitments have been made against the category, and the present balance is prepared by a business office and forwarded to the project director. This type of report is not particularly useful for management because the manager cannot tell whether or not he is spending too quickly, too slowly, or appropriately. Successful project management requires the manager to know at all times the rate and level of expenditures. He must have a method of budget preparation which will help him develop a planned rate and level of expenditure against which he can compare his actual rate and level.

A MANAGEMENT APPROACH TO BUDGETING

Most of the project management systems that have been developed have focused primarily upon time or schedule. Costs are planned and accounted for in an almost independent manner. With the development of project management systems for the planning and controlling of time in research and development projects, attempts to integrate both time and cost were begun. The integration of cost resulted in a new method of budgeting. The essential feature of the new budgeting procedure is the shift in emphasis from *inputs* to *outputs*. The relation of cost to work to be accomplished is now heavily emphasized. Since most work can be planned and controlled in a time dimension, the costs necessary for this work can be determined accordingly, and the project definition phase can provide an account of funds spent.

The basic vehicle in the planning and controlling of costs becomes the project definition or workbreakdown structure outlined in Chapter 5. The workbreakdown structure identifies several major components of work leading to the accomplishment of the final objective. Each of these components, under the budgeting procedure, is called a *summary end item* and receives a *summary number*. Each end item is further divided into components called *work packages*. Each work package is assigned a *charge number*. Figure 9.2 illustrates this procedure. Direct costs are charged only to *charge number* items or work packages. These work packages are also referred to as *cost centers*. In order to obtain the cost of a summary end item, the charges belonging to the work package are totaled. Sometimes there may be intermediate summary items and numbers between the summary end item and the work packages. These intermediate numbers represent different levels of the workbreakdown structure, and are given for the use of different levels of management. Their computation depends upon the information requirements at these levels. The normal procedure is to total directly from work package to summary end item without computing intermediate totals.

In estimating costs, the personnel, materials, services, travel and other direct costs needed to accomplish the work package are determined. The estimation can be done at the work package level, or at a more detailed level by determining the costs associated with each

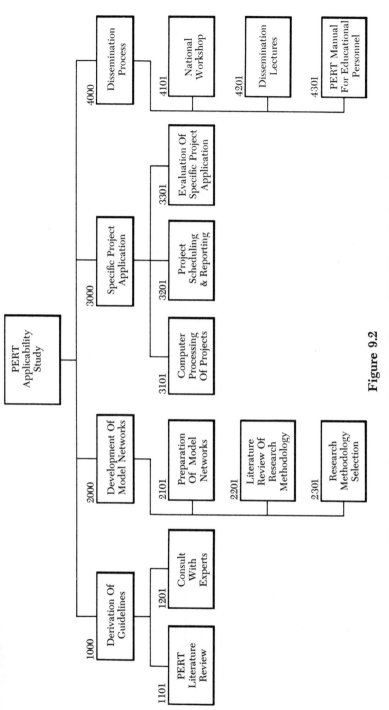

Figure 9.2

Illustration Of Account Numbers Charged To Work Packages And End Items.

151

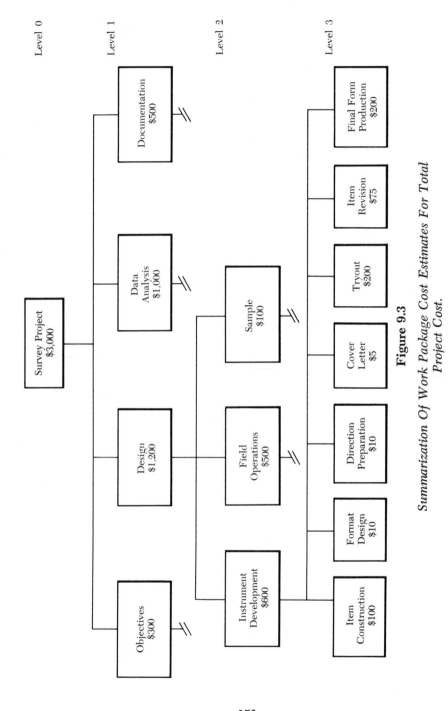

Figure 9.3

Summarization Of Work Package Cost Estimates For Total Project Cost.

activity in the work package and totalling the individual costs. If the project is small, this may be the procedure to use. If the project is large, estimation at the individual activity level may be awkward. A modified outline of the procedure is shown in Figure 9.3 for a simple survey project. In this case, a "shopping list" of activities has been identified and cost estimates established for each one. These costs are then totalled to form the estimated cost for the work package, and the costs for the work packages are then totalled to provide an estimated cost for the project.

A more detailed budget may be prepared by using the form illustrated in Figure 9.4. The worksheet shown in the figure is for personnel but similar sheets can be prepared for other budget categories. The work sheet is completed by identifying the work package with its preceding and succeeding event numbers and indicating the type of personnel required for the work, using a rate figure for their services and the amount of time they are needed. These two items are multiplied to secure a total cost figure. The portions of the total cost to be supplied by the funding agency and the contracting institution are then decided. Finally, the information on the personnel worksheet can be transferred to the traditional budget format. The worksheets developed in planning the budget can serve as a means of comparing actual spending against planned personnel spending in a work package. Cost estimations for a work package, or activity, should be made by the personnel and manager who will be responsible for doing the activity or work package.

The estimating form is relatively simple. It can be made more complex to show more detail. It also can be designed to handle computer processing of cost estimates. However, the size and complexity of most educational research and development projects, at the present time, does not require computer processing of cost estimates using complicated forms. The costs of computer processing are consistent with the benefits derived from it. In these forms, materials and other costs can be entered directly, while personnel estimates can be shown in the form of estimated hours, days, and months using accompanying resource codes. Most established organizations have a resource code book for various personnel which gives an hourly cost figure that includes base pay, fringe benefits and other costs. These forms that estimate personnel requirements by resource code rather than time or schedule requirements make it easier to adjust personnel requirements, if it becomes necessary. The procedure also helps to control the project since it can be easily converted into a planned

South West Institute
for
New Developments and Leadership in Education
1000 Ermac Avenue
Cook City, Piedmont
00006
Worksheet A—Personnel

Work Package (1) P. S.	Description (2)	Rate (3)	Time (4)	Requested from Agency (5)	SWINDLE Contribution (6)

TOTALS

Transfer Totals From Columns 5 and 6 To Budget Summary Sheet

Figure 9.4

Worksheet For Preparing Work Package Costs.

actual cost report, and expenditure rate curves can be established for each work package by using the schedule start and end dates.

This procedure is related to direct costs, and there remains the question of indirect costs. Several methods have been used to handle indirect costs. One method determines the direct cost figure and then adds a fixed percentage for indirect costs. Another method determines the fixed and variable components of indirect costs and charges only the costs which are variable (i.e., attributable to the actions of the work packages) to the work package. In this case, variable indirect costs become a form of direct costs. Fixed indirect costs are combined and charged to the entire project or split between several projects within the organization. This method of handling indirect costs is more detailed and difficult to implement but it does allow for more precise control. The use of either approach depends upon the project manager's need for the information and control.

One final point should be made about this second method. The work package is the basic costing unit, but sometimes an indirect cost can be totally attributed to the three or four work packages which combine to form a summary end item. In this case, a "dummy" work package can be developed to accumulate these costs and insure that they are totaled only to the summary item rather than spread throughout the project. In some cases, this type of work package has been given the title "General Support Services."

A major advantage of the work package and activity costing method lies in its development of an enumerative cost model. Various costs are directly related to specific activities and periods of time. This permits the integration of time-cost relationships in control reports, and gives the project manager a clearer picture of the project's status. The work package costing method also breaks a complex project into units which are easier to visualize. While errors can be expected, their magnitude should decrease. This method, however, requires a change in accounting methods which management may not want to undertake and explains why the method is not being rapidly adopted. This is a limitation for control purposes but does not preclude its use in the cost estimation process.

A Summary of Budgeting Problems

The value of a budget as a planning and control device should be obvious. There are several problems, however, which make a budget less effective than it is designed to be.

Budgeting is an interactive process as are the other phases of planning. A budget should not be prepared simply by adding the totals established for each work package or a project. The individual responsible for a work package should be sure that the funds he receives will cover the cost of any emergency, or will allow him freedom of action in completing his responsibilities. Simply totalling these requests may result in a figure above any level of funding. The interactive process should result in a final budget request that is realistic. Each work package request should be reviewed for its consistency with other work package requests and the overall project requirements. Hopefully the review process will discover errors in estimation and correct them.

The person responsible for budget preparation should be prepared to justify any amount of funds requested. Many problems can be avoided if, during the preparation of the budget, time and attention are given to the justification process. The funding agency should know exactly what is needed, why it is needed, how much needed, and what rate it is needed. For example, a request might take the form of "three hours on IBM 360 at $400/hour for questionnaire processing." In the case of personnel, a justification might take the form "Associate Director, 100 percent time for 18 months at annual salary rate of $13,000 per year." The inclusion of this type of justification makes it easier for the reader of the budget to know exactly how the money will be utilized when it is available.

Earmarked funds are a problem. Budget categories may be so inflexible that an excess in one cannot be adjusted by a smaller amount in another. Shifting funds also entails problems, so there is no one satisfactory solution to this difficulty.

If the budget is to be an effective control device, the manager who controls both the schedule and performance criteria, must also control the budget. Project control is always a balance between the time, cost, and performance.

There are various contractual problems associated with many budgets. Some contracts limit the amount of travel and expense reimbursement. These limitations may, in turn, limit the availability of certain consultants. There also may be severe restrictions on equipment purchases. Depending on the importance of the equipment, this could be a nuisance when equipment rental is the only alternative.

Another problem may be described as a "funds flow matching" problem. That is, contract funds may be allocated in segments, dependent upon the receipt of progress reports. If the reporting period does not correspond with the accounting period, incoming funds may not be received at the time that project expenses must be paid.

The uncertainty that exists in research projects makes budgeting difficult. This problem can be alleviated to some extent by a variable budget contract. That is, no fixed amount is determined but the organization is assured of having its expenses covered up to a specified limit. This type of budget is typical of defense R & D projects but is not as widely used in educational research.

A final problem centers on the disparity between what is on paper and what is actually done. The project manager must first teach his personnel what a budget is and how to develop it. He then must force his personnel to use the budget. The budget, as a planning document, will only be an academic exercise if it is not used for control.

Check List for Cost Estimation and Budget Preparation

Listed below are several questions which should be asked in preparing the cost estimates and budget, in order to be sure that the significant points have been covered before the project is submitted for funding.

1. Have cost estimates been assigned to *work* or the production of products rather than to *functions*?

2. Have salary increases and fringe benefits for future years been considered?

3. Has the indirect cost rate been determined and/or secured?

4. Have the guidelines issued by the funding agency been carefully checked for items which can or cannot be included in the budget?

5. Has the type of contract under which the project will be funded been determined?

6. Do the line items which appear in the traditional budget format have an adequate "justification" or explanation?

7. Has there been a check made to determine if there is sufficient information from past experience which can help in making estimates for a current activity?

References

1. Baumgartner, John S., *Project Management*. Homewood, Ill.: Richard D. Irwin, Inc., 1963.
2. Clarke, R. W., "Activity Costing—Key to Progress in Critical Path Analysis," *IRE Transactions on Engineering Management*, Vol. EM-10 (September 1963), pp. 132-36.
3. _____, "Nature of the Time-Cost Relationship," Graduate School of Business, Stanford University, California, 1961.
4. Dilley, Frank B., "Program Budgeting in the University Setting," *Educational Record*, XLVII, No. 4 (Fall, 1966), pp. 474-89.
5. Dykeman, F. C., *Financial Reporting Systems and Techniques*. Englewood Cliffs, N.J.: Prentice Hall, 1969.
6. Hollister, Robinson G. Jr., "A Decision-Making Budget," *Educational Record*, No. 4 (Fall, 1966), pp. 490-97.
7. Johnson, Robert W., *Financial Management*. Boston: Allyn and Bacon, Inc., 1966.
8. *PERT/COST, System Design*, DOD and NASA Guide, 0-646214, Washington, D.C.: U.S. Government Printing Office, 1962.
9. Shillinglaw, Gordon, *Cost Accounting*. Homewood, Ill.: Richard D. Irwin, Inc., 1967.
10. Vaizey J. and J. D. Chesswas, *The Costing of Educational Plans*. UNESCO International Institute for Educational Planning, 1967.
11. Villers, Raymond, *Research and Development Planning and Control*. New York, Financial Executives Research Foundation, Inc., 1964.

chapter 10

Project Control

It was noted in Chapter 2 that planning and controlling are emphasized in educational project management. The five previous chapters in Part II have dealt with the sequence of steps that should be undertaken to develop the initial plan for a project. Many of these steps are repetitive, and several revisions of the project plan may be needed before it is acceptable to the project management. The sequence of steps should preceed the actual writing of the formal research and development proposal. A careful explication of project goals and work flow as well as schedules and budgets can help to make a more realistic and readable proposal.

If an individual develops and anticipates the implementation of a plan, he also implies that the plan will be controlled. If the control function is exercised by an agency, it can be assumed that a plan does exist. Implementing a plan without related control usually results in the unsatisfactory conduct of the plan. This chapter will describe the nature of the control function, and its relationship to initial planning efforts, and monitoring operations once the project is under way. For convenience, the chapter has been divided into a section dealing with the concept of control and

159

a second section dealing with the activities carried out by the project manager in putting the control operations into effect.

THE CONCEPT OF CONTROL

There are, perhaps, as many definitions and explanations of control as there are authors writing about the topic. Koontz and O'Donnell (16) indicate that control involves being sure that what is done is the thing one intended to do. Lindberg (16) indicates that the principal function of control is to make things happen. A useful definition of control has been presented by Ackoff (1). He states that planning consists of establishing a set of initial decisions and control consists of reviewing and revising these decisions as necessary in order to accomplish the plan. This procedure may require many original decisions to be modified during the course of the project. This is not surprising, as most plans are modified between the time they are conceived and their completion. More simply, control is an action which adjusts operations to predetermined standards. It is this idea of adjusting operations to predetermined standards that establishes the relationship between planning and controlling. The steps concerning time, cost, and performance taken in planning establish the predetermined standards to which conditions are adjusted during the operation of the project. Because planning establishes the standards, control is constrained by quality of planning. If there is a precise plan, the potential for accurate control is enhanced. Conversely, if the plan is not precise, control cannot be carried out properly.

The conditions under which planning and controlling occur also need to be considered. Planning usually occurs in a rather leisurely situation while control occurs under conditions of urgency. If the plan miscarries once it is implemented, there is frequently little time to correct the situation. Because of the difference in the two situations, it is important to consider control as the plan is developed. By doing so, many potential trouble spots can be eliminated, and management can be provided with more time to react to problems.

The Control Formula

With these ideas of the concept of control as background, generalized procedures for management control can be developed. Most authors on management control agree that the following four points must be considered in establishing successful control.

1. The development of effective standards or criteria against which actual performance can be judged
2. The placing of these standards at strategic points since it is the points that are to be controlled and not the processes
3. The development and creation of some monitoring procedure in order to compare performance to standards
4. The establishment of some procedure for correcting the deviations that occur between performance and standards

Kepner and Tregoe's (14) statement of "shoulds" and "actuals" help to establish what is involved in control. The initial plan establishes what *should* be happening. Control, which is usually in either written or oral form, determines what is *actually* happening, compares it to the plan, and takes the necessary corrective actions.

These four steps form what might be called the *control formula,* and would involve:

1. Adopting a plan that establishes time, cost, performance standards
2. Measuring and reporting progress against those standards
3. Noting deviations from standards and taking corrective actions
4. Implementing corrective actions by recycling the plan as needed

A scheduled completion date of a project element is an easier standard against which to compare deviations than a performance standard involving attitudes toward a new instructional program. In order to properly control a performance standard, the manager would need a carefully defined criteria regarding the attitudes that are acceptable.

Comparisons between planned standards and actual conditions are *measurement* problems and susceptible to the usual problems associated with the quantifications of tasks and behaviors. Unfortunately, therefore, control is frequently limited to what can be easily measured. Feedback is also another problem since the manager must be able to receive information about a situation rapidly but clearly. The project information system should first establish the types of information desired by management. The feedback or monitoring system should provide management with up-to-date information about situations for which decisions have to be made.

Control is exercised at *points* in the project. It is not possible to plan and control processes, but points of accomplishment can be planned and controlled. This idea is applied, for example, in network analysis by assigning schedule dates to events, since these represent points in time. The daily expenditure of funds cannot be controlled, but total dollar cost at a particular point in time for a particular item being produced can be controlled. The process of item writing in a test development project cannot be controlled *per se*. We can, however, control the number and quality of items produced by noting the percent that have to be rejected because of their poor item statistics. Our standard for the item writing process might be a less than ten percent rejection rate. One of the major problems in the control operation is the establishment of those points at which control will be exercised. The process of establishing these points is closely related to the process of establishing standards and measurement previously discussed.

There are other dimensions of control that need to be examined. One problem concerns *what* should be controlled. In general, the major elements of time, cost, and performance need to be controlled. The manager should have a means for controlling all three dimensions at one point in time, but practical limitations may preclude his gathering data on all three elements at one time.

Another problem is *how much* control should be exercised. The amount of control employed at a particular point depends upon the work being performed, the individual performing it, and the organizational structure. Neither over control which exists when operations are too closely monitored, nor under control which occurs when operations are to loosely monitored will help project completion.

The third problem is *who* should control. Control usually should parallel the distribution of authority and responsibility in the organization. The person charged with the responsibility for an operation should also be charged with controlling that operation. It is a recognized principle of management that decisions should be made at the lowest authority level. The same principle also applies to control, but because of the legal responsibilities of the project director and his organization, many final decisions will have to be made by him rather than the person responsible for the job.

The fourth problem concerns the types of information presented to management. Data is considered as raw, unstructured, unedited elements and therefore of little use to managers. Information is data which has been structured, summarized, and edited so that it conveys some meaning to the manager. Managers can receive too much information. Managers should receive the minimum amount of information needed for optimum decision-making. Computers and similar devices have helped to have information summarized and presented to managers quickly. Unfortunately, they have also caused managers to receive more information than they really need. The primary value of the computer lies in its capacity to provide information quickly so that action can be taken while the problem is small.

This section might best be summarized by asking the question of *why* control? Control helps to make the most efficient use of the resources. Both time and money are limited, and performance is closely related to these two factors. The initial planning effort strives for resource efficiency, and control is an extension of this attempt. Since plans are rarely carried out without problems or deviations, control is necessary if there is serious concern about the implementation of a plan. Furthermore, control helps to eliminate or minimize potential problems. Careful planning will help to eliminate some problems. But, in many cases, it cannot be carried out effectively because the manager is overwhelmed with current problems. Sometimes, managers are unable or fail to see weak spots in their plans. Unless involved in the planning, a manager may not see the complexity of a plan. For these reasons, control plays an important role in successful project management.

The subsequent sections of this chapter outline the activities involved in successful project control. For purposes of discussion, three major activities have been identified. The first is the process of reporting, the second is management actions, and the third is implementing management actions. These three specific activities are the general operations carried out in the control process. The reader should be familiar with each activity so that he can handle problems involving all three activities. Reports may not be prepared, or prepared badly, or if prepared, management may not pay any attention to them. Management may pay attention to the report and take corrective action, but the action or decision may not be implemented. In order to have proper control, all three activities must be fully considered and carried out.

NATURE AND FUNCTION OF MANAGEMENT REPORTS

A control system provides the manager with information, usually in the form of oral or written report, that compares the actual performance to planned performance. There are two types of control systems, the closed loop and the open loop system. In the closed loop system, deviations between the actual and planned performances result in the immediate implementation of automatic rules and structured courses of action. In the open loop system, automatic rules and structured courses of action do not exist or exist at a minimum level. These systems are used when they are unique, important, and nonrecurring deviations. These two systems are somewhat analogous to the types of decisions that Simon refers to as *programmed* and *nonprogrammed* decisions. Both control systems will exist within projects. Both systems require that management is informed of any deviations so that either automatic rules can be applied or problem analysis undertaken in order to arrive at a solution to the problem.

Regardless of the control system employed, reports are necessary. Personal contact, meetings, and presentations are often used to carry out the control function. While highly desirable as means of communications in small projects, these types of reports become difficult and less efficient in a larger project or organization. Consequently, a reporting system that can meet the information needs of managers and utilize some type of standard format should be developed. The primary consideration in designing reports for management involves several principles which are discussed below.

Report Design Requirements

A report should be understandable and convenient. A manager should be able to see immediately the status of a situation, and the trouble spots and errors needing action or attention. Consequently, management reports should employ graphic procedures. These graphic reports should be in a form that highlights discrepancies or deviations. Gore (9) presents a good discussion of how "briefings" can be used as a way of communicating reports to project management.

A report should always compare actual progress against planned progress, planned expenditures against actual expenditures, and planned performance against actual performance. Without these comparisons the report is not useful to management.

In addition to reporting actual conditions and planned conditions, a report should also predict future progress or status. Attention should be given to what is currently happening and what will happen in the future.

Management should be able to see whether their previous corrective actions have improved the situation. This will enable the manager to study the effect of his decisions as well as the decisions of subordinates. It provides an objective basis for personal performance appraisals.

Finally, the report should provide management with only those deviations that can be considered "exceptions". For this reason, management reports usually deal with extreme situations since only the deviations beyond the pre-established boundary are called to the management's attention for action.

Progress and Final Reports

The most common types of reports are the progress and final report. The funding agency usually requires a progress report at periodic intervals and establishes the guidelines for its preparation. These reports should provide useful information to the funding agency which can then help the project manager to complete his work successfully. However, in reality many of these reports are not useful.

The report developed periodically by the project staff for its own use is the most typical kind of progress report. How often this report is prepared depends upon management's desire or need to control project elements. Some elements can be monitored daily. Others can be monitored weekly, monthly, or perhaps even yearly in long duration projects. Report preparation takes time, so there should be a balance between the cost of preparation and management's need for the report. Progress reports can hide bad situations as well as expose them. This often occurs if subordinates fear a punitive reaction. Management should prevent this type of situation from arising.

The final report is a summary of all the activities and operations carried on during the project and may include a report on the technical results of the work. The guidelines for a project's final report are usually established by the funding agency, and funds are often provided for its preparation.

Illustrative Reports

In an ideal situation, progress reports indicate the present compared to the planned conditions in cost and performance. In most practical situations, each element is reported on a individual basis. Some of the problems associated with an illustrative report are presented below.

The ability to report actual time or schedules against planned time or schedules depends upon the validity of the schedule established for the project. In many cases, it may be difficult to measure progress in a particular task. This fact highlights a need for control points. While we cannot measure the actual progress in writing a book, we can measure, for example, progress in terms of the scheduled dates that were set for the completion of the first draft, the revised draft, and the final publication. We can compare actual progress against these planned dates, or *points*, and note the deviations from them.

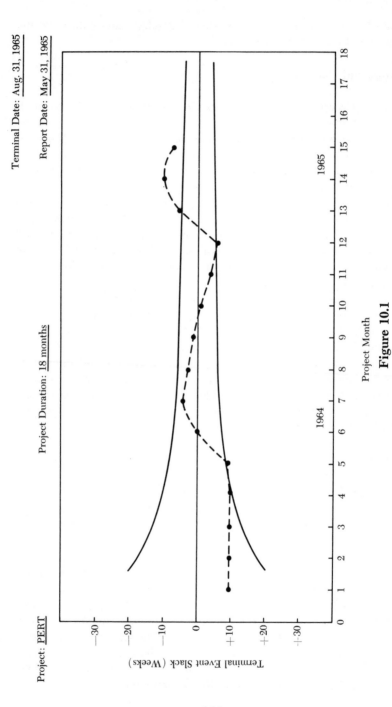

Project: PERT

Project Duration: 18 months

Terminal Date: Aug. 31, 1965

Report Date: May 31, 1965

Figure 10.1

Project Schedule Outlook Report.

Figure 10.1 illustrates a schedule report chart that plots the slack condition associated with the final event of a project. In this figure, the slack condition noted at the end of each month is plotted over the total duration time of the project. In the early months of the project a positive slack condition existed which gradually moved into a negative slack condtiion, followed by a return to a positive slack condition. This condition was followed by an extreme negative slack towards the end of the project. Also shown in the figure are boundary lines which widen at the beginning of the project but narrow toward the end of it. This cone shaped boundary line reflects the fact that larger deviations are permitted early in the project since there is still time to correct them. As long as the deviations remain within these boundary lines, the project manager is willing to accept them. This type of situation, however, is not be true toward the end of the project when the extreme negative deviation occurred.

In addition to illustrating progress, other reports can show further detail about internal milestone events or points of the project. Figure 10.2 represents a common type of chart referred to as a milestone report or an E-L-Chart. On the left, the milestone events have been listed, and, on the right, a calendar plots the earliest scheduled completion date (represented by a black triangle) and the latest allowable scheduled date (represented by a white triangle). As long as the black triangle, representing the earliest expected completion date, preceeds the white triangle, representing the latest allowable completion date, there is not much concern for management. If the white triangle should preceed the black triangle, then it is a problem for management attention.

The reporting of planned versus actual expenditures can be shown in a manner similar to the two previous illustrations. Instead of showing positive or negative slack conditions on the left or vertical axis, projected over-runs and under-runs of the budget against time can be shown. Similar types of boundary lines can also be applied. A chart similar to the milestone event report could be created, except that the planned and actual expenditures for various work tasks using the work packages would be shown. Figures 10.3 and 10.4 illustrate these two types of charts. The major problem in demonstrating planned versus actual costs is ensuring that the planned expenditures have been divided into tasks, since total actual expenditures do not indicate whether or not certain project segments have over-committed future funds.

The measuring and reporting of performance is, perhaps, the most difficult task in project management. There is no present system that

Project: __PERT__

Report Date: __March 1, 1964__

Event Number	Event	1964 1-1	2-1	3-1	4-1	5-1	6-1	7-1	8-1	9-1	10-1	11-1	12-1	1965 1-1
002	Project Approved			▲	△									
004	Begin Guidelines			▲	△									
040	Begin Project Selection			▲				△						
010	Begin Workshop Plans			▲										
019	Begin Workshop				▲									
000	Begin Dissemination Plans			▲										
001	Guidelines Completed							▲	△					
030	Begin Manual Preparation							▲	△					
003	Model Networks Developed								◪		△			
036	Manual Completed													
010	Project Applications Eval'd											△		
027	Dissem. Lectures Completed													
085	Final Report Completed													

Figure 10.2

Project Internal Milestone Event Report.

168

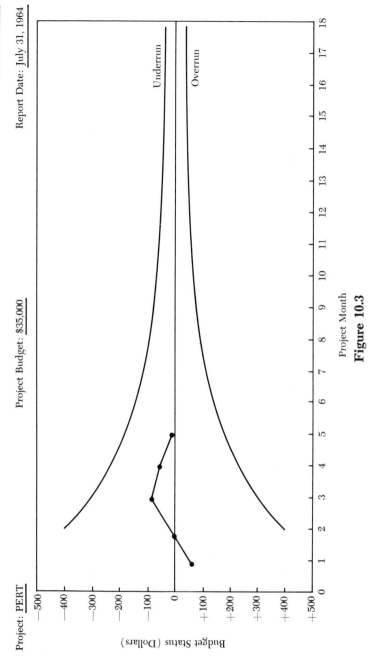

Figure 10.3

Project Budget Outlook Report.

169

Project: PERT Project

Page: 1 of 5

Summary Cost Center: Dissemination Lectures

Report Date: 6/31/65

Work Package P. Event—016 Succ. Event—070		Plan To Date	Actual To Date	Over (Under)	Action
Number	Item				
100	Materials Preparation	$ 300	$ 400	100	▲
200	Travel	$2,000	$1,500	(500)	▲
300	Materials Mailing	$ 50	$ 50	–	△
400	Visual Preparation	$ 150	$ 175	25	▲
	TOTALS	$2,500	$2,125		

Action Code: △ —No Management Action ▲ —Needed Management Action

Figure 10.4

Project Work Package Cost Report.

is satisfactory. A rigid definition of standards is the best way to ensure quality output and to provide a vehicle for comparisons of planned and actual performance. It is helpful to identify the variables which need to be controlled. Figure 10.5 illustrates this approach. In this figure the reliability and validity coefficients are to be controlled as

PROJECT: Test Development   SCHEDULED DATE: 4-29-68

VARIABLE	ESTIMATED VALUE	TOLERANCE	ACTUAL VALUE	DEVIATION
RELIABILITY COEFFICIENT	.80	$\pm$ .05	.79	$-$ .01
VALIDITY COEFFICIENT	.70	$\pm$ .05	.60	$-$ .10

Figure 10.5

Illustration Of Performance Report.

the test is developed. In the planning stage, certain estimated values are set for each variable as well as the boundary lines within which deviations may occur. After the initial test is developed, we compare the actual values with those that we had estimated. While the reliability coefficient is acceptable, the validity coefficient is not. The manager must now decide what to do about the validity coefficient. Unfortunately, he cannot decide until he sees the time and cost reports. There is, therefore a need for a integrated time, cost and performance reporting system.

Recognizing the need for a integrated system, we have illustrated in Figure 10.6 how this type of system would operate. In this illustration, the work package is a test that will be used in a subsequent part of the project. In the left column, there is a series of time, cost, and performance variables, or points, that are to be monitored. On the right side of the illustration, the planned standards are shown as well as the actual status. For example, the scheduled date for completion was March 17, while the actual completion date was March 18 which was probably within acceptable deviation limits. The original cost for the result of the tests was estimated to be $100, but the actual cost was $150. There was a $50 over-run which was a potential prob-

PROJECT: Test Development
WORK PACKAGE: Initial Test

REPORT DATE: 3-20-69

	VARIABLE	PLAN	LIMITS	ACTUAL	DEVIATION	ACTION
TIME	Milestone Event–020 Scheduled Date	3/17/69	± 1 wk.	3/18/69	—	△
COST	Total Budget for Work Package	$ 100	—	$ 150	+ 50	▲
PERFORMANCE	1. Reliability Coefficient	.90	± .05	.90	—	△
	2. Validity Coefficient	.80	± .05	.70	− .10	▲
	3. Average Student Time to Take Test	60"	—	80"	+ 20"	▲
	4. Percent Students Understanding Sample Exercise	100%	− 5%	100%	—	△
	ACTION CODE:	△ NO MANAGEMENT ACTION		▲ NEEDED MANAGEMENT ACTION		

Figure 10.6

Illustrative Integrated Management Report.

172

lem. In the performance dimension, there was interest not only in the reliability and validity coefficients but also the average time taken by students to complete the test, as well as the percentage of students who understood the sample exercise provided. At the time of the report, the reliability coefficient was acceptable but the validity coefficient was below standard. The average time taken by the students exceeded the planned time, but the students fully understood the practical exercise. A managerial examination of this report would show the potential problems in the budget over-run, the decreased validity coefficient, and the exceeded time limits.

Before discussing possible management actions, it should be pointed out that reports for management vary with the level of management involved. Usually, reports prepared for high level management contain only vital information and focus upon milestone events within a project. Reports prepared for operating units and project divisions contain more detail. The general information flow in management levels is upward and tends to become more condensed. Several network analysis techniques, like PERT and CPM, have received wide acceptance, because they have successfully integrated and generated the detailed time and cost information needed for all levels of project management.

Up-Dating or Preparing to Report

The process of preparing a report for management is referred to as *up-dating*. Up-dating involves an examination of the project status on a "time-now" basis. It occurs immediately before reports are sent to management according to their schedule for reporting or upon special request. The actual time period involved in the up-dating process is short, usually not much longer than a 24 hour period, since the report will give the most current status of the project operations. It is in securing this rapid status report that the computer becomes useful for processing of data. Up-dating involves three major categories of project tasks:

1. Past: what has happened to date
2. Present: what is currently going on
3. Future: what has yet to be done

The first major task in up-dating is the identification of the activities which have been completed and the events which have been reached since the last report period. In an initial report, it would be the task and events which have occurred since the project was started. Completion dates for these events are noted and compared to scheduled dates. Task times are recorded and compared to actual times to improve future estimations. Some reports are prepared and show all the work completed to date, while others delete the information which does not immediately concern management. This information, however, can provide the manager with an idea of why current activities are running behind schedule.

The second major task is to determine what activities are currently in progress. Having identified them and keeping in mind that for any activity in progress, some original scheduled time has passed, estimates for the remaining completion time required are secured from the person or unit responsible for the task. These estimates can be either deterministic or probabilistic. It is possible to include in these estimates needed or desired revisions of work tasks or even possible reallocation of resources.

The third major task is to secure information about work which is not yet begun. The original tasks can be re-examined and new estimates secured if desired. At this point, the manager can consider readjusting the work flow in terms of what has happened or is happening in the project. Like the original estimates, the activities and time estimates for jobs not yet started are essentially forecasts regarding the future.

In addition to the above types of data and information, other information such as a new ending date for the project, changes in resource allocations, or changes in objectives, which need to come to the attention of the manager can be incorporated into the report. Once the information is assembled, the data is processed by hand or computer and should reflect current project status. The results of the processing can then be prepared in visual displays.

The up-dating routine should provide several levels of management with the best possible report of the present status of the project in terms of time, cost and performance.

MANAGEMENT ACTIONS

Having received the prepared report, management takes action based upon the conditions the report has established. This section will outline the general tasks that face management, if actions appropriate to situations presented in their report are going to be taken. For convenience, the section has been divided into three topics, problem analysis, generation of alternative solutions, and making a decision.

Problem Analysis

Since a report compares planned to actual progress, discrepancies, either positive or negative, are usually present. Usually reasons for the deviations exist. Kepner and Tregoe (14) have suggested that, in most cases, a deviation occurs because there was some unplanned change. In order to take corrective action, it is necessary to know the exact nature of the deviation, when it occurred, how serious it is, and where it occurred. Management should try to identify the *reason* why the change occurred. Unless the reason can be determined, any proposed solution will probably be inappropriate. Therefore, project managers should quickly develop problem-solving skills, including the ability to specify the nature of the problem. The manager may have to test alternative hypotheses of causation before deciding what factor caused the deviation.

Generation of Alternative Solutions

Having identified the problem and its cause, the manager must generate possible solutions for restoring the situation to the planned condition. In order to adequately evaluate the alternative solutions, the manager must know what his objective is in making the decision. For example, if his objective is to return the project to schedule without concern for cost and performance, then one set of alternatives can be generated. If his concern is to restore performance without concern for time and cost then another set of alternatives can be generated. In short, the manager must know the objective of his decision. Having established the objective of the decision, he can generate alternative actions and test them against the objective. Numerous techniques have been devised to assist the manager in comparing alternatives and objectives. An adequate solution depends upon the number and quality of the alternatives. At this point, project personnel familiar with the problem can provide useful alternatives since they have most intimate knowledge of the problem and its possible solutions. However, frequently the individuals familiar with the problems cannot generate new approaches or alternatives. Consequently, it is not unusual to use both experts in the problem area and outside consultants in order to have the best possible alternatives.

Before the final decision is made, the manager must consider the possible adverse consequences of the decision. That is, the various alternatives should be tested for what might happen if they were employed. At this point, the simulation of alternative solutions is useful and demonstrates the advantage of network analysis. In network analysis, alternative solutions can be run through the computer until a satisfactory condition is established.

Making a Decision

Finally, the manager announces his decision and communicates it to the staff and department members involved. The decision is only a human judgment regardless of the information available, or the expertise of the consultants. The manager tries to accumulate the information he needs, generate reasonable and feasible alternatives, study the adverse consequences of a possible decision, and then choose a course of actions.

These steps can be assisted by reports from the individuals associated with the problem. Figure 10.7 is an illustration of the kind of report that could be presented to management.

The problem presented in the illustration occurred in a real project. The original schedule date for the project was August 31, 1965, and the report date was May 31, 1965. An up-date of the project revealed that approximately twenty-five weeks were required to reach the final event. Twelve weeks alone were required for the art work, planning and preparation of the final report, which was to be a published monograph. This situation delayed the final report by a total of eleven weeks. Once the problem was presented to the staff, a meeting was held to discuss the possible alternatives. Three alternatives are shown in the illustration, but more could be generated for a particular problem. The alternatives were considered in terms of replanning, costing, and time gain. The two recommendations presented to the project director concerned the reduction of the art work, and the simplification of the art work. Either alternative might have gained the necessary time or, at least, reduced the severity of the problem. The project director decided to reduce and simplify the art work but not eliminate it entirely. The objective guiding the decision was a preference for maintaining the project's time schedule for the manuscript and a willingness to sacrifice what might be called a performance dimension of the project.

The form illustrated in Figure 10.7 could be used to represent a variety of the problems. It could be used as a supplement to the project outlook report and milestone event charts. It could be supplemented by a more detailed document discussing the nature of the

PROJECT: *PERT*

TERMINAL DATE: 8-31-65
REPORT DATE: 5-21-65

PROBLEM ANALYSIS	IMPACT	MANAGE-MENT GOAL	POSSIBLE ALTERNATIVES	RECOMMENDED ACTIONS	MANAGEMENT DECISION
PROBLEM: Total of 25.6 weeks required to submit final report. According to present plan, 12.7 weeks are required for art work planning and preparation.	Delay of final report submitted by 11 weeks.	Turn final report in on time and within present budget.	1. Request time extension 2. Re-evaluate art work requirements 3. Re-evaluate estimated times for present art activities.	1. Reduce and eliminate selected art work 2. Simplify art work to be used	Simplify art work to be included
PROBLEM:					
PROBLEM:					

Figure 10.7

Illustrative Problem Analysis Report.

problem and the possible alternative solutions considered by the project staff. Presentation of the problem and its possible solutions in this form enables the staff to deal directly with the problem since it is highlighted for management action.

Implementation of Management Decision

Once the manager has decided upon a course of action, it must be communicated to the staff and other members involved in the project. Necessary adjustments should be made in the project definition, work flow, schedules and resource allocation as well as budget. Because of the frequent changes which occur during a project's life span, it is useful to maintain the project work flow on a glasine covered cardboard so that changes can be incorporated easily by using a cloth and grease pencil. A record of management decisions that change a network flow can be recorded in a format similar to that presented in Figure 10.8. This chart shows the existing work prior to a management decision and the work flow that occurs as a consequence of the management decision. Similar charts might be created for cost and performance decisions. Management should institute follow-up procedures to ensure that the decision has been incorporated and the necessary adjustments have been made.

CONTROL PROBLEMS

The control system must point out quickly the deviations from the plans so that the manager can take actions to correct these deviations. The major problem here is the possibility of delay between the occurrence of a deviation and its report to the manager. Kottler (17) has indicated several types of delays that might occur within a control system.

These four types are illustrated in Figure 10.9. A deviation may occur, but there may be an information delay between the time it occurs and the time it is reported. Subsequently, there might be a decision delay between the time a deviation is reported and a new plan developed. There might then be an implementation delay between the time the new plan is developed and the time that it is implemented. This might be followed by an impact delay between the time the new plan is implemented and the deviation occurs. One of the dimensions of improving control systems is to improve the possible information and action delay conditions in the project.

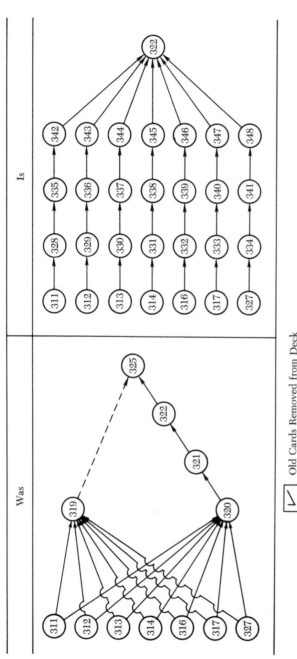

Figure 10.8

Illustration Of "Was-Is" Chart.

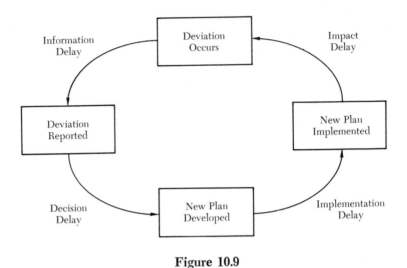

Figure 10.9

Delay Possibilities In A Control System. (After Kottler.)

It is important that the project manager recognize that the general steps about the nature of control reporting systems, management actions, and implementation of management decisions, will continue throughout the course of the project. Early in the project effort the problems of control and how they may be effectively handled should be given careful consideration.

Check List for Project Control System

Listed below are several questions which the project manager should consider in establishing and operating the control system for a project.

1. Who shall receive what reports?

2. Have I developed a procedure which enables me to up-date the project prior to the preparation of status reports?

3. Do different components of the project need different report schedules?

4. Shall I have separate time, cost, and performance reports or combine them into an integrated report?

5. Do my report forms contain sections which compare planned to actual progress?

6. Have I established criteria and standards for each objective?

7. Have I established limits for each control point so that if a deviation exceeds that limit management action is called for?

8. How formal and informal does the report system need to be?

9. Does the staff sufficiently realize the need to report significant deviations promptly and accurately?

10. Do my report forms emphasize visual presentation of project status or are they principally narrative and verbal?

11. What are progress report requirements from the funding agency? Final Report Requirements?

12. Have I developed a means or vehicle for the identification of problems, determination of problem causation, the creation of alternatives, and the selection of a solution choice?

13. What consideration has been given to the primary criteria for decisions that have to be made? Major objectives of any decisions?

14. Have I set up a procedure for holding staff meetings in order to discuss progress reports and deal with problem areas?

15. Do the staff and I operate under the management by exception principle?

16. Have I developed a means for implementing decisions?

17. Has there been developed a means for documenting changes made in the project plan for purposes of a historical record?

18. Has a procedure or process been developed for communicating to concerned staff members the changes made in the project plan?

References

1. Ackoff, Russell, *A Concept of Corporate Planning.* New York: Inter-science Publishers, Inc., 1970.
2. Anthony, Robert N., *Planning and Control Systems: A Framework for Analysis.* Division of Research, Graduate School of Business Administration, Cambridge, Mass.: Harvard University, 1965.
3. Baumgartner, John S., *Project Management.* Homewood, Ill.: Richard D. Irwin, Inc., 1963.
4. Beer, Stafford, *Decision and Control.* New York: John Wiley & Sons, Inc., 1966.
5. Blau, Peter M., and Richard W. Scott, *Formal Organizations: A Comparative Approach.* San Francisco: Chandler Publishing Co., 1962.
6. Bonini, C. P. (ed.), *Management Controls: New Directions in Basic Research.* New York: McGraw-Hill Book Company, 1964.
7. Drucker, P. F., *The Effective Executive.* New York: Harper & Row, Publishers, 1967, Chapters 6 and 7.
8. Dykeman, F. C., *Financial Reporting Systems and Techniques.* Englewood Cliffs, N. J.: Prentice Hall, Inc., 1969.
9. Fried, Louis, "Executive Controls," *Management Services,* V, No. 3 (May, 1968), pp. 17-26.
10. Gamer, W. F., "Fitting Operations Control Reports to Management Needs," *Management Services,* VII No. 2 (March, 1969), pp. 38-43.
11. Gore, J. B., *Briefing as a Method for Communicating Reports to Project Management.* Unpublished Master's Thesis, Columbus, Ohio: Ohio State University, 1969.

12. Greenwood, William T. (ed.), *Devision Theory and Information Systems.* Cincinnati, Ohio: South-Western Publishing Company, 1969.
13. Head, Robert V., "Management Information Systems: A Critical Appraisal," *Datamation* XIII, No. 5 (May, 1967), pp. 22-27.
14. Kepner, C. H. and B. B. Tregoe, *The Rational Manager.* New York: McGraw-Hill Book Company, 1965.
15. Koontz, Harold and Cyril O'Donnell, *Management: Book of Readings.* New York: McGraw-Hill Book Company, 1964.
16. _____, *Principles of Management.* New York: McGraw-Hill Book Company, 1964.
17. Kottler, Philip, *Marketing Management.* Englewood Cliffs, N. J.: Prentice Hall, Inc., 1967.
18. Lemke, B. C. and James D. Edwards, *Administrative Control and Executive Action.* Columbus, Ohio: Charles E. Merrill Publishing Co., 1961.
19. Lindberg, Roy B., "The Unfamiliar Art of Controlling," *Management Services,* VI, No. 3 (May, 1969), pp. 15-20.
20. McNeil, John F., "Program Control Systems," *IEEE Transactions on Engineering Management,* Vol. EM-11 (March, 1964), pp. 29-42.
21. *PERT/COST Output Reports,* Supplement No. 1 to DOD and NASA Guide, PERT Coordinating Group, (March, 1963).
22. Robinson, David M., *Writing Reports for Management.* Columbus, Ohio: Charles E. Merrill Publishing Company, 1969.
23. Schoderbek, P. P., "Is PERT/COST Dead?," *Management Services,* V, No. 4 (November, 1968), pp. 43-50.
24. Thornley, G., *Critical Path Analysis in Practice: Collected Papers on Project Control.* London: Tavistock Press, 1968.
25. Woodgate, H. S., *Planning by Network.* London: Business Publications Limited, 1964.

chapter 11

A Generalized Project Management Model

The preceeding chapters have described the nature of activities that a project manager must carry out to develop an initial project plan and maintain operational control of the project. This chapter will present a model system for project management which utilizes the principal ideas presented in the previous chapters.

The model has been derived from a study of the functions and operations in existing management systems, the author's experience in management, instructional programs on management systems, and an analysis of the existing literature on the problems and procedures involved in project management. The model does not represent any particular existing management system although many of the concepts that are present in management systems have been incorporated.

Through a study of the generalized model, a project manager can develop his management system, utilizing all or parts of the model. It is hoped that by using selected general systems concepts and principles, the reader can become familiar with these concepts and their use in an actual application.

Before presenting the model, which was identified in the introduction to Part II with the acronym PACT for Planning and Controlling Technique, it would be beneficial to outline some general criteria for judging a model management system. One source (4) has set forth desirable criteria for use in appraising any management system but particularly project management systems. The criteria are presented so that the model can be judged against them to determine its validiy. The specific criteria take the form listed below. Paraphrasing the statements in the original source, it can be said that a good management system does the following:

1. provides timely, pertinent, adequate, and accurate information to the manager
2. assures that decisions are made in advance of performance
3. forces effective planning before the initiation of the project
4. must be flexible to accommodate necessary changes
5. must be simple in operation and understandable by all users
6. must be economical
7. must permit management by exception
8. must provide a basis to evaluate courses of action prior to initiation
9. must forecast trouble spots and indicate current deficiencies
10. must indicate significant differences between planned and actual performance.

OUTLINE OF A PROJECT MANAGEMENT MODEL

A project management system should develop an initial plan for a project which includes time, cost, and performance specifications. It should also provide a vehicle for monitoring and controlling the operation once the project is initiated.

The total system function is accomplished by establishing and developing two major subsystems which relate to the management functions of planning and controlling. A summary of a model developed from these two functions is shown in Figure 11.1. The total model system is divided into three major elements. The Planning System and its component parts is shown at the top of the diagram. The Control System and its major components is shown at the bottom of the figure. Located between these two systems is a box identified as the Project Data/Information Base. Solid arrow lines indicated the general flow of work, while dotted arrow lines represent the flow of information. A study of the figure will show that information is gen-

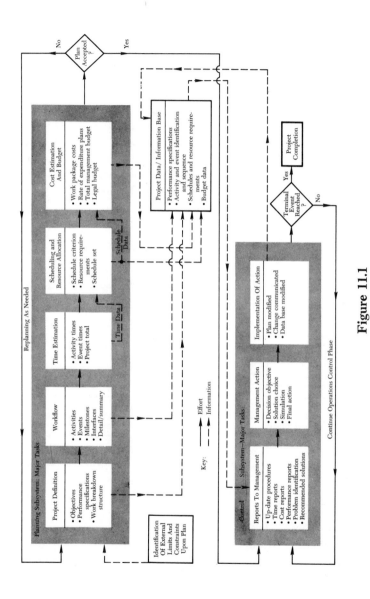

Figure 11.1

*PACT—A Management System For Planning And Controlling
Of Projects.*

187

erated during each of the tasks in the planning stage, and this information is fed into the data base box. The data base box becomes the basis for management reports since it indicates what items management plans to receive information about during the project. As changes are made in the project plan in the operational phase, new information and data are generated and fed into the information/data base. Also illustrated are the conditions of repetition in both planning and controlling. In planning, the process goes on until the plan is accepted. In controlling, the process goes on until the final event of the project. A project proposal in narrative form would be a plan, and the information contained in the document would become the data base for that project. Understanding the relationship between planning, the project proposal, and the data/information base will help the manager of the project to develop a better control operation.

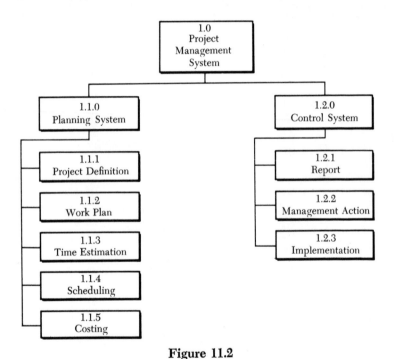

Figure 11.2

Outline Of Model Project Management System.

The division of the total model system into two subsystems of planning and control is somewhat arbitrary and artificial, as Anthony (1) has stated in his discussion of planning and controlling systems.

Control is carried out continuously, even during the planning phases. Decisions also are made continuously during the course of the project. We will break these management functions into somewhat arbitrary categories in order to focus on a particular function. The categorization into a planning and control system is done to highlight the task of developing an initial plan and the task of making subsequent adjustments during the project operations.

Planning Subsystem

The Planning Subsystem provides an initial plan for the accomplishment of the prime project objective as well as its supporting objectives. It also provides a data base which can be utilized by the project manager in the control function.

To accomplish the initial plan, the functions and subsystems relating to project definitions, work flow, time estimation, scheduling and resource allocation, and cost/budget estimates must be identified. Each of these functions is discussed below.

Control Subsystem

The control system provides management with timely, relevant, and valid information so that problems can be identified, alternative corrective solutions considered, and decisions made and implemented by recycling the project as needed.

To accomplish this function, three separate subfunctions and appropriate subsystems can be identified. These functions and subsystems relate to report preparation, management actions and decisions, and implementation of management decision or recycling.

Outline of Systems Components

A hierarchial outline of the overall model presented in Figure 11.1 is shown in Figure 11.2. Each of the components discussed in subsequent pages of this chapter have been numbered to correspond to their placement in each of the major systems of planning and controlling. Thus the project definition component is numbered 1.1.1 to show that it is a sub-unit of the Planning System numbered 1.1.0.

Each of the components of the two major components of the model is described in terms of its functions, needed inputs, general process or sequence steps, and the output generated at each stage. The reader should carefully study each of the components in order to derive full benefit from the model. In the inputs section of each phrase, certain information as well as needed skills are identified. A prospective manager should be competent in these skills in order to use the model effectively.

1.1.0 *Planning Subsystem*:

1.1.1 *Project Definition*

Subsystem Function: The function of this subsystem is to establish the boundaries of the project by developing a hierarchially ordered structure of the major and subordinate objectives which reflect work that has to be accomplished to reach the overall goal of the project and which are expressed as products or functions along with performance specifications or criteria of their accomplishment.

Input	Sequence	Output
1. Major project objectives	1. Develop mission statement or overall project goal	Project definition in form of work breakdown structure in graphic or tabular form which is product or function oriented
2. Knowledge of system concepts		
3. Production/Function decision	2. Identify major end items to accomplish step 1	
4. Known limits and constraints	3. Develop subordinate tasks to major end items in step 2	
5. Desired or stated performance specifications	4. Assign responsibility for work package development	
6. Knowledge of processes involved in establishing objectives and criteria of accomplishment	5. Determine criteria for work package accomplishment 1 through 5	
	6. Review and revise as necessary	
	7. Management approval	
	8. Reproduce	

1.1.0 *Planning Subsystem:*

1.1.2 *Work Flow*

Subsystem Function: The function of the work flow subsystem is to develop a graphical representation of the logical sequence of the activities and events necessary to accomplish the objectives identified in the project definition subsystem taking into account necessary interrelationships, dependencies, and constraints.

Input	Sequence	Output
1. Project definition 2. Rules for work flow plan to be used (Gantt, network, etc.)	1. Develop overall work flow using milestone events 2. Establish interface events	Project work flow in chart from (network) showing summary and detailed work flows
3. Computer use decision 4. Milestone events 5. Task/event numbering decision 6. Event coding system (milestone, interface etc.)	3. Assign responsibility for work package flow development 4. Develop detailed work flow 5. Check for rule violations 6. Check final logic of work plan 7. Revise as needed 8. Adopt task identification scheme (event numbering) 9. Management approval 10. Reproduction work plan	

1.1.0 *Planning Subsystem*:

1.1.3 *Time Estimation*

Subsystem Function: The function of this subsystem is to provide information regarding estimated total project completion time, earliest and latest start and finish time for the initiation and completion of individual work tasks, slack or free time, and critical path.

Input	Sequence	Output
1. Knowledge of deterministic or probabilistic estimating procedures	1. Secure and record estimates for individual activities	Work flow showing initial terminal time, milestone time, critical path, slack paths and individual task times
2. Work flow	2. Assign final date if known to terminal task or master plan	
3. Directed or schedule dates if known		
	3. Assign scheduled date to milestones if known	
4. Persons to provide estimates		
5. Work sheets	4. Calculate expected activity times	
6. Knowledge of permissible re-planning procedures	5. Calculate earliest task completion time	
7. Knowledge of probability theory	6. Calculate latest allowable completion time	
8. Prior knowledge of job task times if available	7. Establish critical path and slack	
	8. Adjust to directed and scheduled dates as needed	
9. Computer program	9. Management approval	
10. Directed or schedule dates if known	10. Finalize	

1.1.0 *Planning Subsystem:*

1.1.4 *Scheduling and Resource Allocation*

Subsystem Function: The function of this subsystem is to establish a schedule for the project by translating the planned schedule derived from time estimation subsystem into specific calendar dates for the initiation and completion of work compatible with resource availability and other known or stated constraints.

Input	Sequence	Output
1. Resource survey	1. Develop functional charts (Gantt or Bar Charts) showing critical path, slack paths, and job sequence	Work flow adjusted to meet resource availability showing start and completion dates for task accomplishment consistent with estimated or directed completion date
2. Decision on schedule criterion		
3. Calendar considerations		
4. Organizational personnel policies	2. Determine resource needs for task accomplishment	
5. Contractor requirements		
6. Final task and milestone dates, if known	3. Adjust task flow as needed to fit resource availability	
7. Determination if a time or resource constraint situation	4. Check against criterion	
	5. Revise as needed	
	6. Translate to calendar dates	
	7. Management approval	
	8. Issue work authorizations	

1.1.0 *Planning Subsystem*:

1.1.5 *Cost/Budget Estimation*

Subsystem Function: The function of this system is to generate cost estimates and a budget or future expenditure plan which provides for the necessary funds needed to accomplish the project as outlined and established in prior subsystems and to provide a basis for future decisions as well as control of current expenditures.

Input	Sequence	Output
1. Scheduled work plan	1. Estimate costs for individual tasks	Budget for project showing costs and planned expenditure curves for major work tasks plus traditional budget categories
2. Project definition	2. Estimate costs for work package using information from step 1	
3. Individual work tasks of work packages		
	3. Summarize costs upwards through project definition	
4. Organizational policies on costs (travel, etc.)		
	4. Develop traditional category budget using data from steps 1 and/or 2	
5. Knowledge of budgeting concepts		
6. Negotiated indirect cost rates	5. Calculate direct and indirect costs figures	
	6. Establish planned rate of expenditure curves for work packages and total project	
	7. Management approval	
	8. Reproduce	

1.2.0 *Control Subsystem:*

1.2.1 *Reports to Management*

Subsystem Function: The function of this system is to provide continuous, accurate, and rapid detailed and/or summary information to appropriate management levels which reflect current project status, and highlights present and potential problems in a form that is concise and clear.

Input	Sequence	Output
1. Data base from planning system	1. Note activities and events completed	Periodic reports to management levels showing project status, problem areas, impact of problems, and suggested alternatives and/or recommended corrective actions
2. Report formats	2. Reestimate as needed time/cost/performance for activities in progress	
3. Briefing techniques		
4. Decision on management levels to receive reports	3. Reevaluate time/cost/performance for activities not yet started	
5. Report dates	4. Process data	
6. Up-dating procedures for organization	5. Analyze outputs for deviations	
7. Deviation limits	6. Identify problems, show impact, develop alternatives with concerned unit	
8. Problem identification skills and concepts		
9. Duties and functions of network analyst	7. Prepare visual reports with accompanying narrative	
10. Report cycles	8. Forward to appropriate management levels	

1.2.0 *Control Subsystem*:

1.2.2 *Management Action*

Subsystem Function: The function of this system is to enable managers at various levels to develop actions and make those decisions which will resolve problems, to correct deviations from original plans, and/or to modify the original plan as desired.

Input	Sequence	Output
1. Management reports	1. Set problems priority	Decisions reflecting solution to be employed to correct deviations or modify as needed
2. Knowledge of decision processes	2. Identify and test causes	
3. Authority and responsibility for decisions	3. Develop objectives for decisions	
4. Contractor requirements if appropriate	4. Establish "musts" and "wants"	
5. Knowledge of problem solving skills	5. Develop and secure information for each alternative	
	6. Eliminate alternatives on go/no-go basis	
	7. Study desirability of possible alternatives via simulation	
	8. Study adverse consequences	
	9. Look for potential problems	
	10. Make decision	

1.2.0 *Control Subsystem*:

1.2.3 *Implementation of Action*

Subsystem Function: The function of the system is to provide a means of implementing management decisions, revising plans, and developing modified data/information base.

Input	Sequence	Output
1. Management decisions 2. Methods of disseminating or communicating management decisions 3. Was/is worksheets 4. Initial or previously revised plans	1. Transmit management decisions to appropriate unit 2. Modify original plans 3. Complete "was/is" worksheet 4. Process new data	Revised plan reflecting adjusted time/cost/performance dimensions as of present and future dates

References

1. Anthony, R. N., *Planning and Control Systems: A Framework for Analysis.* Cambridge, Mass.: Harvard University, Division of Research, Graduate School of Business Administration, 1965.
2. Cook, Desmond L., *A Generalized Project Management Model.* Educational Program Management Center, College of Education, Columbus, Ohio: Ohio State University, 1968.
3. _____, "The Use of Systems Analysis and Management Systems in Project Planning and Evaluation," *Socio-Economic Planning Sciences,* II, No. 2, 3, 4 (April, 1969), pp. 389-97.
4. *Program Evaluation and Review Technique,* Army Material Command Regulation 11-29, Headquarters, U. S. Army Material Command, 1966.

part 3

Organizational Considerations and Projects

The two previous sections have dealt with the project manager's role and how he can successfully plan and control a project. Projects operate within organizational structures. This section will present some of the issues and procedures involved in project selection within an organizational structure and the factors that relate to the successful implementation of project management systems.

chapter 12

Project Selection and Termination

Until now, we have been concerned with the general concepts and principles of management and specific problems in project planning and control. It has been assumed that the reader will find this knowledge of immediate and practical value. In other words, we have assumed that a project already exists. In this chapter we shall discuss the general problems and procedures in selecting a project from competing projects as well as terminating a project once underway.

IMPORTANCE OF ADEQUATE PROJECT SELECTION

Almost every organization has only limited resources for the various programs and projects that it undertakes. Researchers and other persons are often able to generate more proposals than there are funds to support them. Consequently, some proposals will be accepted, while others will be rejected. The organization, however, must recognize that if all available resources are allocated to a few projects, its ability to respond to new ideas is limited. It must not only be concerned with funding present and proposed projects but also future projects which have not yet been identified. All three types of projects will drain available resources. The projects selected or rejected may affect the success of the agency, or organization. It becomes a matter of developing procedures and criteria on which to base the selection and evaluation of proposals and their control once they are begun.

It is generally accepted that project research and development is a most expeditious way to accomplish a task. Consequently, any system, agency, or organization concerned with the administration of research and development must provide some policies and procedures to help guide the selection of projects. They must have techniques and procedures for the initiation of ideas, methods of selection, development of proposals, evaluation of proposals, review of projects in progress, and the termination of projects. Unless these techniques exist, projects may be selected in a haphazard manner and create unwanted problems in their administration.

Most of the research and development work relating to procedures for project selection has been done in the industrial area because the market value of research and development are important considerations of the organization. Some investigations, however, have been carried out in military, government, non-profit foundations, and other agencies which sponsor or fund project activities. From the operations of these agencies, several steps in project selection can be identified. Baker and Pound (2) provide the best paper on the techniques and procedures used in the research and development of project selection. In addition to Baker and Pound's discussion, Hertz and Carlson (9) provide an excellent discussion of the relationship between project selection and planning. From their point of view, research projects should relate to long-range planning while product-and-process projects should relate to short-range planning. Rubenstein (18) provides an excellent discussion of the research currently carried out in the project selection process. He summarizes the situation by pointing out that in any research and development activity one must avoid failing to undertake *good* projects and instead undertaking *bad* projects. The following procedures for project selection developed from practice, research, and experience are designed to prevent either of these two errors.

General Processes in Project Selection

Figure 12.1 presents four stages of project selection as well as some of the activities that might occur within each stage (9). The first stage, *conception,* concerns the procedures and techniques for generating research and developing ideas. It includes some simple statement of the idea, perhaps not more than a paragraph or two, and its placement on a list of existing ideas. Out of this stage may come some type of rough priority of ideas which may interest or concern the company. The next stage, *feasibility,* involves a review of the existing literature to see if the idea has been done before, consultation with staff members to discover what they know about the project and its possibilities, consideration of its appropriateness to organizational goals and objectives, and attention to its possible significance for education. Again, a rough ordering of projects in terms of their merits can be established at this stage. The third stage, *definition,* assumes that the two previous steps have met with organizational approval. The detailed proposal is prepared and a technical review provided. In this stage the most vigorous screening of the idea occurs. Included in the review are sections on how the results will be disseminated as well as the costs benefits inherent in the project. From this stage, evolves some type of priority for funding.

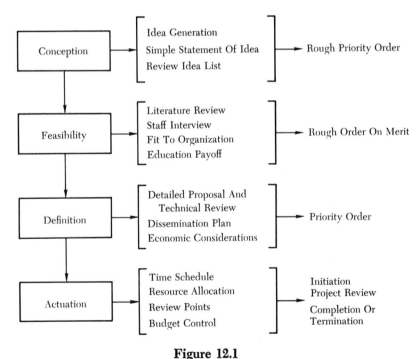

Figure 12.1

General Steps in Project Initiation And Selection.

If the project survives these three steps, it is ready for the fourth step, *actuation*. This step involves the actual ability to initiate the project and includes a time schedule, resource allocation for the project, the establishment of review points, and budget control. During the actuation phase, projects are reviewed periodically. Depending upon the results of the review, the projects are allowed to continue or are terminated. Any new project is judged against other current projects within the organization. Consequently, the proposed idea has to meet a rigid screening process in order to receive any funds.

Criteria for Project Evaluation

In addition to the research on project initiation and selection, much research has been done on the criteria that should be used to judge whether or not a particular proposal will be approved, deferred, or rejected. A set of project evaluation criteria which were developed for the selection of research projects under the Cooperative Research Program of the U. S. Office of Education is shown below.

CRITERIA FOR THE EVALUATION OF PROPOSALS
FOR RESEARCH UNDER P. L. 531, U. S. Office of Education

Educational Significance

1. The proposed research, survey, or demonstration is concerned with the development of new knowledge directly applicable to the educational process or with new applications of existing knowledge to problems in education.

2. The project is focused primarily on educational problems of major importance.

3. Primary consideration is given to new projects or to those where duplications can be defined as a scientific check on previous assumptions or conclusions.

4. The anticipated outcomes of the project are of potential value to education on a nation-wide basis.

Research Design

5. The problem with which the research proposes to deal is clearly defined.

6. The proposal reflects an adequate knowledge of other research related to the problem.

7. The questions to be answered and/or hypotheses to be tested are well formulated and clearly stated.

8. The proposal outlines fully the procedures to be followed and wherever applicable, includes information on such points as sampling procedures, controls, types of data to be gathered, and statistical analyses to be made.

Personnel and Facilities

9. The director or principal investigator is someone who has previously done research in the area involved and/or who has clearly demonstrated competence for directing work in that area.

10. The plan provides, wherever feasible, for encouraging and increasing research knowledge and skills of professional personnel and of new research workers.

11. The institution or agency submitting the proposal has facilities generally adequate for carrying out the research.

Economic Efficiency

12. The suggested approach to the problem is reasonable in terms of overall cost as compared with the cost of other possible approaches.

13. There is a favorable relationship between the probable outcomes of the project and the total expenditure in terms of overall value.

It is assumed that the specific criteria listed under each general category, as well as the general categories themselves are relevant criteria upon which to judge the proposal.

A review of these criteria leads to three categories of factors upon which projects are rated. The first category concerns the *significance* of the study. This category considers potential usefulness of the results and their relationship to existing knowledge in the field. It is an attempt to determine whether or not the problem is important to education and will produce results that can be generalized. A second major category is *financial*, and concerns the cost of the project not only in terms of dollars but also in terms of potential return on the investment. The third category is *technical considerations*. Factors such as the chances for success, the qualifications of the personnel, and the state of procedures to be employed are considered.

Once a set of criteria has been established, projects can be reviewed and evaluated. Usually review and evaluation procedures can be divided into *qualitative* and *quantitative* methods. This dichotomy is somewhat artificial, but it does provide a way of categorizng the selection procedures. Giving a numerical value to the factors that are rated does not necessarily improve the results or make the methods quantitative, as the qualitative element remains.

Qualitative methods usually focus upon factors such as the reputation of the proposal initiator, but even may be on a first-come, first-serve basis. In certain scientific fields, money for research is provided solely on the basis of the principal investigator's reputation. In some cases, the funding agency feels that his skills will eventually produce a good project.

The most common procedure is quantitative and involves the basic principles of decision theory. In this procedure, the various projects under consideration are assumed to be independent of each other. The major proposal elements such as objectives, procedures, personnel, are rated numerically on criteria presumed to be related to project success. These elements of the rating scale can either be weighted or unweighted. A total score for the project is then established. Decisions regarding funding are usually made within some type of budget constraint. For example, seven of ten projects under consideration may be found acceptable and rated above a minimum numerical value for funding. After the projects are rated, an examination is made of the available funds to determine how many of the approved seven will be contracted immediately and how many might wait for later funding. This procedure is frequently used in the field of education.

More sophisticated approaches are used within business and industry. Many of these involve quantification in some form of economic analysis or operation research approach. For example, for a series of alternative projects, factors such as development, cost, probability of success, and related variables are estimated. The projects are selected by maximizing net value of the project, subject to the availability of things such as raw materials, manpower available, total budget, and facilities. These procedures become highly quantified in operation and are not widely used in the social and behavioral sciences, where the economic reward is not as easily determined.

Within the qualitative and quantitative approaches, the most common procedure for project selection used by public funding agencies such as the U. S. Office of Education and National Science Foundation is the use of "field readers" who provide ratings of projects, using criteria and forms developed for this purpose. Lists of these "readers" are maintained by the agencies and reflect the areas of expertise and competence needed for proposals submitted to that agency. Proposals are forwarded to the reader who provides their evaluation and recommends approval or disapproval. It is common to employ as many as five readers for a particular proposal. The results are summarized by the funding agency who then decides whether or not to offer funds. This procedure can produce interesting situations when field readers disagree over the worth of the proposal. In these cases, it is often the funding agency that resolves the situation, and, in some cases, it becomes a single person's judgment.

Some agencies not only employ field readers but also arrange for the field readers to meet as a group after providing independent ratings. Proposals are discussed, differences resolved, and some type of group decision reached. This procedure offers several advantages. Face-to-face discussions of points at issue can be held and differences resolved more effectively. Furthermore, it does not result in a single person making a decision because of discrepant evaluations.

It is possible through a study of the project management process to become a more critical reviewer of proposals. Proposals submitted for review will be carefully scrutinized to see how the time, cost, and performance elements of the proposal relate. In some cases, it can prevent an under-budgeted project from being funded at the requested level when a review of the work indicates that a higher level of funding is needed. However this knowledge can also prevent an over-budgeted project from being approved in view of the time and work involved. Potential project proposal reviewers should have some kind of training program in project management so that better project ratings can be made.

Reasons for Project Disapproval

A discussion of project selection procedures should also offer some indications of why projects are not approved. Several studies have been made of this problem and reports published. A typical example is that presented by Allen (1). Making a study of 605 research grant applications which were submitted during a two month period, he classified the reasons for rejection into four major categories of *problem, approach, man,* and *other*. In the *problem* area, the most frequent reason for disapproval was lack of importance or doubtful production of any new or useful information. Within the *approach* category, the most common reason for disapproval was that the proposed test methods or procedures were unsuited to the state of objectives. Sometimes, the description of the approach was too nebulous and lacking in clarity to permit accurate evaluation. In the *personnel* category, the major reasons were the investigator's lack of experience or training, or the researcher's unfamiliarity with recent literature pertaining, or the researcher's unfamiliarity with recent literature pertaining to the topic or methods used in previous work. In the other category, the most common reason was that the requirements for equipment or personnel or both were unrealistic.

Smith (20), in reviewing proposals submitted to the Cooperative Research Program of the U. S. Office of Education, cited several frequent reasons why proposals were rejected. Among these were that the problem was trivial or unrelated to education, the problem was not delimited, the objectives or hypotheses were stated too broadly, the procedures were lacking in detail, a simple design was used to investigate a complex problem, and relevant variables were not considered or were lightly dismissed. Many funding agencies explain to the proposal initiator why the project was rejected. This information can be valuable to a potential investigator when he submits later projects. In some cases, projects are initially disapproved but a request is made for resubmission with corrections. When this happens, it is because the idea is recognized as significant, but certain methodological problems exist, that need to be clarified or strengthened. When this is done, the project may be funded.

Project Termination

Under normal circumstances, projects once funded are allowed to run to completion. There are occasions when, however, there may be a need to terminate a project. The decision to terminate is difficult because it is possible that a promising project will be ended although success is near. It is not possible to establish quantitative or objective guidelines for termination. Decisions about termination may best operate on a probability basis. That is, based upon present evidence of project status, it appears that the success is not likely. One might consider, under these circumstances, a temporary termination and a subsequent re-funding when the situation is more favorable, or there has been a change in goals, or the staff has become available.

An interesting set of criteria has recently been provided by Buell (4), based upon the idea that one cannot establish specific criteria for termination but can use certain warning signals that suggest that termination is desirable. Among the signals he identifies are the following:

1. The practicality of the goals of the project.
2. Administrative support for the project.
3. The project team is stalled and grasping at straws.

4. The project does not have the right kind of personnel.
5. Prior researchers have already explored the project's possibilitis.
6. Loss of key personnel.
7. The project staff lacks enthusiasm.

It has sometimes been suggested that selected milestones should be established for a project when possible termination is considered. In these cases, reviews are made at the milestone points, and if the work has not been successful, termination is considered in order to transfer the allocated funds to other or new projects. Occasionally, there has been voluntary termination because of no significant success, but this appears to be an unusual circumstance.

Project Selection Problem Areas

Even though much time and energy has been given to improving the process of project selection, certain problems continually face agencies or individuals involved in project selection.

Project selection is similar to investing in the stock market. One has to sense, evaluate, compare, and choose from the investment opportunities that exist. If sufficient information is available, these opportunities are valuable. However, some losses can occur. Many of the individuals writing about project selction approach it from an investment opportunity viewpoint. Research should be done to improve these investment opportunities by providing more and better information about each project.

The nature of the research and development process itself confuses project selection. Projects that have specific objectives tend to secure favorable attention since objectives, procedures, and similar items can be more explicitly stated. Projects in an area of research that is not specific tend to be unfavorably received by review committees and panels. Consequently, rating a variety of different proposals using the same set of criteria becomes a difficult task. This is not only true in the case of research and development programs but also in the substantive areas. Applying a standard set of criteria to a variety of possible projects becomes an almost impossible task.

Another major problem is the relationship that exists between professional status, roles, promotions, and acceptance or rejection of a project. While specific evidence is not immediately available, it is reasonable to assume that some professional reputations have been established only because the individuals have received project funds.

Other individuals may have been discouraged from research and development actvities simply because numerous attempts to secure funds have failed.

Another problem concerns the joining of project planning to project implementation. In many cases, a project may be planned for a particular time but due to the time of funding, it may be inconvenient to implement the project at that time. Consequently, the successful completion of the project is in jeopardy. A related problem in this area is the need to know that the project carried out is the same one that was planned.

Some investigations of the judgments used in selecting projects show that these judgments are colored by the success of the project at some subsequent time. Research should be done to determine what information is used or needed at the time of the decision. The author has found that comments made by other reviewers strongly influence the final rating given the project even when the reviewers have previously and indpendently rated projects, without prior knowledge of the rating given by other personnel.

Several writers have suggested some research questions related to improving the project selection process. Brandenberg (3) has compiled a list of the problems that need study. Since potential projects may be developed to investigate these problems, the reader might be interested in reviewing the suggested problems. In view of the large amounts of money that are provided in the research and development area, there is a need for research on project selection and termination procedures so that more valid statements can be made about the existing process. In most cases, project selection operates under "rule of thumb" or heuristic procedures based upon general patterns observed in various funding agencies.

Regardless of the source of project selection procedure, it is important to recognize that two risks are involved in any decision to allocate money to a particular project. First, the ultimate benefits may not be as great as expected. Second, an alternative research project, which might have been fruitful, may have to be rejected. When one considers that an individual's reputation and future status may depend upon the approval or disapproval of his project, the decisions regarding project selection in an organization become crucial.

References

1. Allen, Ernest, "Why Are Research Grant Applications Disapproved?," *Science*, CXXXII, No. 140 (November, 1960), pp. 1532-34.
2. Baker, N. R. and W. H. Pound, "R and D Project Selection: Where We Stand," *IIEE Transactions on Engineering Management*, Vol. EM-11 (December, 1964), pp. 124-34.
3. Brandenburg, R. G., "Project Selection in Industrial R and D: Problems and Decision Processes," *Research Program Effectiveness*, M. Yovits, (ed.), New York: Gordon & Breach, Science Publishers, Inc., 1966.
4. Buell, C. K., "When to Terminate a Research and Development Project," *Research Management*, Vol. X (July, 1967), pp. 275-84.
5. Collcut, R. H. and R. D. Reader, "Choosing the Operational Research Program for B.I.S.R.A.," *Operational Research Quarterly*, Vol. XVIII, pp. 219-42.
6. Dean, B. V., *Evaluating, Selecting and Controlling R and D Projects*. Research Study 89, American Management Association, 1968.
7. Hanna, Lyle, *Preparing Proposals for Government Funding*. Englewood Cliffs, N. J.: Prentice-Hall, Inc., 1970.
8. Hartman F. and S. Moglewer, "Allocation of Resources to Research Proposals," *Management Science*, XIV, No. 1 (September, 1967), pp. 85-110.
9. Hertz, David Z. and Phillip G. Carlson, "Selection, Evaluation, and Control of Research and Development Projects" in *Operations Re-*

213

search in Research and Development, B. Dean, (ed.), New York: John Wiley & Sons, Inc., 1963.

10. Kamranz, N. M., *et. al.*, *A Heuristic Investment Model for Nonprofit Research*. Systems Development Corporation, Santa Monica, California, 1966.

11. Mottley C. M. and R. D. Newton, "The Selection of Projects for Industrial Research," *Operations Research*, VII, No. 6 (November, 1959), pp. 740-51.

12. Rankin, Alan C., "The Administrative Process of Contract and Grant Research," *Administrative Science Quarterly*, I, No. 3 (March, 1957), pp. 275-94.

13. Robbins, C. K., *A Management System for Exploratory Development*. Air Force Flight Dynamics Laboratory, Wright-Patterson Air Force Base, Ohio (undated).

14. Roberts, E. B., "How the U. S. Buys Research," *International Science and Technology*, No. 33 (September, 1964), pp. 70-77.

15. Rosenberg, H. H. and H. M. Bain, Jr., *Program Planning for Research and Development in the Navy*. Washington Research Office, Syracuse University, 1964.

16. Rosenfeld, J. M. and Mathew Smith, "R and D Planning in the Decentralized Organization," *Research Management*, Vol. X (November, 1967), pp. 425-38.

17. Rubenstein, A. H., *A Real-Time Study of Information Requirements for Project Selection in Research and Development*. The Technological Institute, Northwestern University, Evanston, Illinois, 1966.

18. _____, "Studies of Project Selection Behavior," in *Operations Research and Development*, B. V. Dean, (ed.), New York: John Wiley & Sons, Inc., 1963.

19. Sacco, W. J., *On the Choice of Long Study Tasks*. Ballistic Research Laboratories, Aberdeen Proving Ground, Maryland, 1965.

20. Smith, Gerald H., *Inadequacies in a Selected Sample of Educational Research Proposals*, Unpublished Ph.D. thesis. Columbia University Teachers College, 1964.

21. Villers, R., *Research and Development: Planning and Control*. Financial Executives Research Foundation, New York, 1964, Chapter 4.

22. Yorke, Allen, Jr., "How Foundations Evaluate Requests," *Foundation New Bulletin of the Foundation Library Center*, IV, No. 4 (July, 1964), pp. 1-4.

chapter 13

Implementing Project
Management Systems

Successful utilization of the tools and techniques for planning and controlling educational research and development projects depends not only upon the user's competency in the particular technique and his mastery of basic concepts and principles but also upon the organizational situation in which the application or implementation takes place. This chapter will discuss some procedures and problems encountered in implementing project management systems. For purposes of presentation, these considerations are categorized as *organizational factors.*

DECISION TO USE SYSTEMS

Before elaborating on these considerations, a more fundamental concern must be discussed. This is the decision made by the organizational unit to implement any particular system or systems. The decision to implement project management systems should be based upon the *need* for them. The need can be determined by dealing with questions such as: what are the objectives in using this system; who will use the system; what are the information needs of the organizational unit; is there a concern with making more effective use of available resources; is there a desire to secure a better coordination between operating departments or functions, and what will be the cost associated with installing a system. The answers to these questions will help the organization to decide whether or not it wants to implement a project or program management system and, if so, what type of system. Once the decision has been made, the procedures and problems that may be encountered in implementing the system or systems should be considered.

Organizational Considerations

One of the major concerns in implementing a project management system, is the need to recognize the problems inherent in introducing a new managment system into an existing organization. The success of the implementation will depend upon how well the objectives are specified for the system as well as the attitudes of the potential users. Woodgate (26) identifies the following objectives as ones that might be considered in implementing a system.

1. to secure better cost planning,
2. to more closely control complex project planning,
3. to make more efficient use of resources,
4. to secure more detailed planning and scheduling,
5. to forecast eventual bottlenecks,
6. to test alternative solutions,
7. to identify a critical activity requiring immediate action,
8. to secure better coordination between operations,
9. to have a better method for planning of uncertainty,
10. to have a method of handling doubts in estimation.

These objectives, either singly or in combination could give direction to the implementation.

The first step for the successful implementation of a project management system is the development and issuance of a *policy statement* from top level management. This will provide an organizational commitment to the use of the systems, including resource commitments. Woodgate has stated that a policy statement might include those projects or situations to which the system would be applied. Results would be expected from the application, the person or department to be placed in charge, the persons and department who will assist and report to the system, and the procedures which will be replaced if in existance. Securing an organizational policy statement, however, is not always easy. Potential implementers must be prepared to demonstrate how the organization can gain from the use of the system.

Once the organizational policy statement is prepared and disseminated, organizational responsibility for implementing the system is assigned. It can be assigned to an existing department, or a special staff can be created. The responsibilities can be centralized or decentralized throughout the organizational unit. The advantages and limitations of the separate staff arrangement in a department utilizing centralized or decentralized approaches are the same as those for any function placed within organizational units. The staff assigned to the implementation can be large or small depending upon the extent or depth of application, the number of projects involved and related factors. The competencies and skills needed by potential staff members are obviously more important than the number of staff personnel. Experience has shown that it is most desirable to seek persons who are interested in the concepts and have the ability to think logically and analytically or have the potential for developing these skills. Potential staff members should be skilled in human relations, since much of their work will involve a variety of individuals.

Once the organizational responsibility has been established, documents about and experience in the types of systems to be employed should be acquired. It is a good idea to develop a professional circulating library of books and periodicals relating to management systems. It is also desirable for potential staff members attend the short courses on project management systems, management information systems, system analysis, and related topics offered by a variety of agencies.

A fourth step is the development of an implementation plan. Time and energy should be given to indicating precisely how the organization will implement the selected management system. The plan should reflect items such as the time at which employees will be trained, and initial decisions regarding computer usage. Many efforts to employ management procedures have failed simply because no one has given enough thought to developing the procedure for establishing the system in the organizational structure. An initial effort could be the development of a plan for the implementation of management systems.

In order to provide consistency throughout the organizational unit, an implementation handbook should be developed. This handbook not only can describe the basic elements of the project management system but also provide certain basic policy statements on implementation. For example, it might cover the symbols to be used in preparing networks, such as milestone event designation, interface event designation, event numbers, and activity descriptions. It could include the types of management reports that are to be made, how frequently they should be made, and what the distribution system for reports will be. Any new staff member joining the organization should be able to receive from the handbook an orientation to the system, and should be able to converse with the system specialist without spending undue time in becoming acquainted with the system.

One of the major factors in successful implementation will be the training given to the staff and other personnel who will be involved in the system. Successful training programs depend upon the knowledge of the personnel conducting the program. The nature of the training program will depend upon the degree of participation in the group. In one experience, the author conducted a one-day orientation session for all members of a state department of education, followed by a week-long training program for selected department heads. The one-day orientation simply informed the staff about the general nature of the system, while the week-long training session provided the needed skills and abilities to those who would be involved in direct usage of the management system. Lectures, films, and other media can be used in the instruction. Experience has demonstrated, however, that adquate provisions should be made for the trainees to work directly with small, practical exercises which will illustrate basic concepts and principles. Usually the instructor can arrange and develop exercises which take the student through project planning techniques step-by-step. These exercises are particularly useful if the orientation time is limited. Should there be an opportunity to extend training time, then it would be valuable to develop an exercise which would have much less structure such as the simulation exercise developed by Dillman and Cook (9). One-day orientations to project management systems should be considered a minimum. A two-and-half day period is necessary for any reasonable coverage of the topic that allows questions. A full week is usually necessary to develop any reasonable amount of skill as well as providing time for the verification of various principles and concepts.

It is important to give time and attention to the presentation of *content*, but equal emphasis should be given to the potential user's understanding of the *processes* involved and the development of *attitudes* favorable to these systems. In some instances, a slightly less than desirable product (i.e., workbreakdown structure, networks) is acceptable, if a desirable attitude can be created. Experience in applying project management systems has shown that forcing potential users to adhere to strict rules often serves as a barrier to successful implementation.

PROBLEMS

The successful implementation of the management systems presented in this book requires the potential user to be aware of the problems that are encountered in the employment of these systems. One major problem involves the resistance to change when transitions to new systems are involved. Many persons are upset and disturbed when the existing system and procedures are abandoned, and new ones employed. The unique nature of project management systems is likely to create some anxiety when terms such as management, planning, and control are used. Misunderstanding these concepts can create emotional reactions which will block successful implementation. In addition to these kinds of resistance, it is not unusual for a person to suggest that the new systems will inhibit their creativity and generation of ideas. This is not the case. In many cases, new systems have helped to bring out creativity since the individuals involved have had a part in the planning activities.

Another problem concerns the integration of a new system into a previously existing system. The need for the new system must be considered and evidence presented that it will produce results. In order to employ the budgeting concepts suggested in this book, two accounting systems may have to be run concurrently, as most present accounting systems do not provide the information needed. Hopefully, it would be possible to develop one compatible system eventually. Correlative with this same idea, is the importance of recognizing that the management systems suggested in this book should not be considered as supplements to intuitive planning and control by the project director. If this approach is held, the author's experience has been that the intuitive system will always be used in a crisis situation because of the processor's need for confidence which he feels in this approach. Unless the project director is willing to work with the system and utilize the information that it produces, there is no point in making the application.

The absence or lack of an implementation plan or insufficient training of participating personnel is another problem. The value of an implementation plan was noted earlier and can only be reinforced at this point. It is also important that the training of the personnel is carried out successfully. Top level management personnel must have more than a superficial acquaintance with any system employed or its potential value will be lost.

The construction of the work flow plan itself or other technical dimensions of the implementation is also important. Usually, management dictates the content and organization of a work plan which does not reflect the actual procedures carried on at the operating level simply because the content is not known to them. Work plans developed by nonoperating personnel may be too idealistic. This same problem can develop when consultants are brought in to help develop the network. A network should never be developed *for* someone. It should be a cooperative effort. The use of consultants does provide an advantage to some individuals, since a system failure can be blamed upon the consultant and not upon the persons using the system.

A desire to benefit from the use of management systems often results in a desire to become operational as soon as possible. Consequently, insufficient time and energies are devoted to proper planning. Potential users of these systems must realize that many phases take a considerable amount of staff time and energy to develop, if they are to be effective management tools. If insufficient time and attention is given to the preliminary work, it may result in a lessening of the system's usefulness. It is not unusual in these situations to have individuals indicate that the technique has little value for them.

Many systems fail simply because the initial applications have not been given enough time. For an initial application of management systems it is best to select some operation with which the participants are familiar and then develop the necessary phases. By operating in this manner, the application can be focused upon the principles and concepts involved, rather than the substantive nature of the situation. After skill and competence have been acquired, one can begin to think of using it with unfamiliar substantive situations. If the intent is to apply the technique to a large project, an initial effort might be directed only to one small part of the project and then expanded as skill and confidence increase. Trying to take on a large job initially can result in a rejection of the system rather than an admission that the users were not ready for the application.

A final source of difficulty lies in problems associated with misunderstandings or difficulty in applying the technique itself. For example, work flow or network construction may involve too much unnecessary detail, or the network may not be laid out well enough so that various pathways can be followed. Initial development of the network can be done best with simple devices such as blackboards and erasers or large sheets of paper and pencils. Many preliminary sketches may have to be made before a final copy is produced which can be drawn by a draftsman and reproduced for display purposes. In other cases, there are technical errors in application, such as a poor selection of milestone events, failure to use the information from management reports, disregarding the timeliness and relevancy of the information, and emphasizing the functions rather than the work. These problems can be overcome if the potential developers and users of project management systems always remember the fundamental objectives of applying such sytsems—those of management planning and controlling.

THE USE OF COMPUTERS

It has been noted earlier in this book that certain aspects of project management systems, for example some rules and guidelines for network construction, are based on the premise that the data associated with the network be processed on computers. When discussing these systems with potential users, the question often arises about whether or not one must use a computer. The answer to the question is dependent upon factors discussed below.

1. *Frequency of Reports.* One major consideration is how often status or progress reports will be desired by management. If reports are desired on a weekly or even daily basis, then the computer is required in order to divide the reports on a rapid basis. If, however, progress reports are only going to be required at less frequent intervals, then perhaps a computer is not as necessary.

2. *Type of Project.* Some projects have a work flow which is well defined and established from past experience while others have a great deal of uncertainty associated with them. In the former case, reports may not be needed as often since there is likely to be less significant deviation. In research activities that have a great deal of uncertainty associated with them, reports may be needed more frequently, particularly in the initial stages so that significant deviations can be corrected or new plans developed.

3. *Duration of the Project.* The total time span covered by a project also relates to potential computer usage. A project covering only a three month interval might be planned and an initial computer processing carried out but no further processing done because of the short duration of the project. A project running for three to five

years would change frequently during the total time, and, therefore, a system of prepared computer reports would be vital to management.

4. *Degree of Complexity.* While it is hard to establish qualified criteria for the complexity of projects, the number of activities and events in a project contributes to a decision about whether or not to use a computer. Usually the more complex the project as exhibited by the number of activities and events (e.g., 200 or more) involved, the more benefit there is in using a computer to assist management.

5. *Cost.* The potential use of the computer must be contrasted in terms of the cost associated with key-punching, computer time, report generation, and related activities with the benefits that would occur for the project director. In some cases, processing the network by hand can be cheaper than utilizing computer processing. Should a principal investigator or project director decide to utilize computer processing but does not have funds to do so, he may want to consider requesting funds for support from the funding agency as part of the project budget.

6. *Facilities Available.* One of the major considerations in utilizing a computer is the characteristics of the computer facility available to the potential user. There has to be a compatibility, for example, between the size of the network and the storage capacity of the computer. The potential user may desire one type of information but the particular computer available and its associated program cannot provide the kind of information desired. If there is any anticipation that a network will be processed on the computer, consideration should be given to its utilization early in the project application so that a decision can be made about proper usage. Almost every major computer manufacturer has some type of network processing program available and are listed in several catalogs (5, 19).

There are many computer programs available for processing networks. Each program has its unique characteristics but some characteristics can be identified for a typical program as shown in Figure 13.1. Most of the programs accept as input data preceding and succeeding event numbers, single or multiple time estimates, activity descriptions, scheduled dates for completion or actual dates of completion, organizational responsibility, sub-network identification, milestone event designation, master schedule events, and similar items. The typical output is harder to describe since there is a great variety and choice in the output formats. Most computer programs, however, print, in standard formats, information relating to the critical path, slack or limited path, expected elapsed time for an activity,

INPUT

Time Estimates
Event Numbers
Activity Descriptions
Scheduled Dates
Directed Dates
State Desired Reports

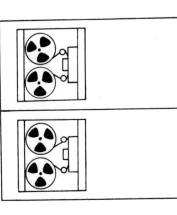

ERROR MESSAGES

Loop Detection
Incomplete Network
Incompatible Dates

OUTPUT

Average Activity Time
Expected Completion Time
Latest Allowable Time
Slack
Critical Path
Limit Paths
Probability
Event and Activity Listing
Master Schedule
Organizational Responsibility
Milestone Reports

Figure 13.1

Typical Computer Processing of Data.

223

earliest expected and latest allowable dates, and probability statements about selected events. In addition, many programs will organize the output so that the information can be readily ascertained. Often a choice can be made about the exact number of activities that one wishes a report to describe. Within one program, the user can request an output report concerning as many as 27 different internal events in the network as well as the final event of the overall project. In addition to input and output information, most programs provide messages regarding errors in networks, incompatible times and date information, and related items.

There are many benefits that can be obtained by using a computer to process network applications. Certainly the speed at which data can be obtained is one of the most significant contributions. This is not only true in terms of updating a project to determine present status but also in terms of the speed that the computer can simulate alternative solutions to problems prior to their actual implementation. Three or four possible alternatives can be considered within a short period of time. The accuracy of the data obtained from the computer, unless the data is input improperly, usually tends to be better than that prepared by individuals. Any data presented to management about the project's status should be accurate and representative of actual project conditions. In addition to speed and accuracy, the computer can assist greatly in the preparation of reports since the output information and data can be structured in many different formats. Some computer programs will print actual bar graphs showing the earliest expected and the latest allowable dates for an activity, the amount of slack, and various related information. These graphical displays can be immediately forwarded to management for consideration.

While the benefits of using computers may be high, there are some limitations which one must consider. First, many people are not familiar with computers and what they can do. Hence, there is an aura of mystery around them and perhaps even a fear of being controlled by them. There must be careful consideration given to a particular computer program. The time and energy employed in using a computer which does not provide useful information is not an effective management procedure. The cost associated with the usage of computers must also be considered. The processing of a network with ten or fifteen activities and events on a computer is a waste of resources. No specific rules have been developed about when one should or should not use a computer, but there appears to be a general consensus that a computer should be employed when the network or work flow reaches about two hundred events or activities. At this point, machine processing is probably cheaper than hand processing.

SUCCESSFUL PROJECT MANAGEMENT IMPLEMENTATION

The emphasis in this chapter, as well as in the entire book, is that project management is a very useful concept and technique for the accomplishment of certain educational research and development activities. The assumption has been that, if the proper attitude is developed and the proper skills are utilized, project management can be successful.

Even under the best statement of intentions, however, there are failures in application. Avots (2) has recently set forth a rather excellent statement of possible reasons for the failure of project management within an organizational setting. It seems appropriate that both the chapter and the book should close by reviewing such reasons, and providing a series of suggestions to aid in preventing this failure.

According to Avots, symptoms of project management failure include situations such as a schedule overruns, high costs, poor quality of end products, excessive design changes, and other similar conditions. He points out that, in some cases, certain projects have failed simply because they should have never been undertaken. But, in most cases of project management failure, specific reasons or causes can be identified. Among the specific causes of failure, six are specified.

1. *The project does not have a sound base.* The reasons for undertaking the project are not clearly stated or there is a failure to recognize the dynamics of the project situation. Projects may be undertaken for the wrong reasons, including the adoption from one environment to another without full study of the variables operating in the two environments.

2. *The wrong person is selected as project manager.* In this case, the person placed in charge has no experience in the substance of the project and/or does not have the necessary managerial skills. The project manager may become too involved with the technical details and not be able to see the overall picture. Hence, the total project slips into undesirable states.

3. *Organizational management is not supportive.* Although a competent man is available, either the company does not subscribe to project management or the man is not provided with the necessary assistance to carry out his many responsibilities.

4. *Inadequate definition of tasks.* Failure to define work relevant to the project from the dimensions of time, cost, and performance is a major factor of project management failure. This point has been repeatedly stressed in this book. All three variables need to be examined together and their relationship must be carefully delineated. A major dimension of this cause focuses upon the situation of asking a project manager to take over the plans developed by someone else. The point has been stressed here that the manager should be identified early and involved in the planning process, as well as in the execution phase.

5. *Misuse of management techniques.* The techniques used to manage the project might either be inappropriate in terms of the project, or be too sophisticated for the staff to understand. For example, the use of probabilistic time estimating procedures brings about a very deterministic project situation. Communication among personnel may also be inadequate, thus leading to unexpected problems or to a failure to inform the staff of top management thinking.

6. *No termination point set for the project.* A project should have a definable end point. In some cases, the project termination point has not been clearly identified. Furthermore, no plans have been made as to staff deployment or to the other organizational adjustments needed when a particular project is terminated.

Recognizing that the above causes need to have remedies, Avots suggests several steps that could be taken to insure project management a successful implementation. The steps he suggests are listed below and will serve as a checklist for the implementation of project management systems for educational activities.

1. When starting off in project management, plan to go all the way.
2. Do not skimp on the project manager's qualifications.
3. Do not spare time and effort in laying out the project groundwork and defining work.
4. Insure that work packages in the project are of proper size.
5. Establish and use network planning techniques, having the network as the focal point of project implementation.
6. Be sure that the information flow related to the project management systems is realistic.
7. Be prepared to continually replan jobs to accommodate frequent changes on dynamic projects.
8. Whenever possible, tie together responsibility, performance, and rewards.

9. Long before a project ends, provide some means for accommodating the employee's personal goals.
10. If mistakes in project implementation have been made, make a fresh try.

References

1. Archibald, R. D. and R. L. Villoria, *Network-Based Management Systems*. New York: John Wiley & Sons, Inc., 1967, Chapters 8, 9, 10, 11 and 17.
2. Avots, I., "Why Does Project Management Fail?", *California Management Review*, XII, No. 1 (Fall, 1969), pp. 77-82.
3. _____, "The Management Side of PERT," *California Management Review*, IV, No. 2 (Winter, 1962), pp. 16-27.
4. Boverie, R. D. "The Practicalities of PERT," *IIEE Transactions on Engineering Management*, X, No. 1 (March, 1963), pp. 3-5.
5. Burns, J. L., *A Catalog of Computer Programs for PERT*. Administrative Services Division, Westinghouse Electric Corporation, Baltimore, Maryland, 1963.
6. Clayton, R. and R. Glenn, "Analysts Look at PERT Through Eyes of the Scientist and the Engineer," *Navy Management Review*, 1962, pp. 12-14.
7. Cook, Desmond L., *PERT: Applications in Education*. Cooperative Research Monograph No. 17, Washington, D. C.: U. S. Office of Education, 1966, Chapter 4.
8. Dillman, D. H., *A Simulation Exercise for the Training of Educational Research and Development Program Managers*, Unpublished Doctoral Dissertation, Columbus, Ohio: Ohio State University, 1969.
9. Dillman D. H. and D. L. Cook, "Simulation in the Training of R and D Project Managers," *Educational Technology*, Vol. IX, No. 5 (May, 1969), pp. 39-43.

10. Feinberg, M. R., "Fourteen Suggestions for Managing Scientific Creativity," *Research Management*, XI, No. 2 (March, 1968), pp. 83-92.

11. Flaks, M. et. al., "Network Management Techniques," *Factory*, Vol. CXXII (March, 1964), pp. 95-112.

12. Francis, R. G., "Practical Advice for the Use of PERT," in G. N. Stillian et. al. *PERT: A New Management Planning and Control Tool*, American Management Association, New York, 1962.

13. Hill, L. S., "Some Possible Pitfalls in the Design and Use of PERT Networking," *Academy of Management Journal*, VIII, No. 2 (June, 1965), pp. 139-45.

14. Kahn, A. B., "Skeletal Structure of PERT and CPA Computer Programs," *Communications of the ACM*, Vol. VII, No. 8 (August 1963), pp. 473-79.

15. Miner, J. B., *Studies in Management Education*. New York: Springer-Verlag New York Inc. 1965.

16. Moder, J. J., and C. R. Phillips, *Project Management with PERT and CPM*. Reinhold Publishing Corp., 1964, Chapters 10 and 11.

17. Olsen, D., "Caution: One Company's Mistakes," *Factory*, CXXII, No. 3 (March, 1964), pp. 95-112.

18. Phillips, C. R., "Fifteen Key Features of Computer Programs for PERT and CPM," *Industrial Engineering*, XV, No. 1 (January, 1964), pp. 14-20.

19. Phillips, C. R. and C. R. Beer, *Computer Programs for PERT and CPM*. Technical Paper No. 13, Operations Research Inc., Silver Springs, Maryland. 1963.

20. Schoderbeek, P., "A Study of the Applications of PERT," *Academy of Management Journal* (September, 1965), pp. 190-210.

21. Schoderbeek, P., "The Sociological Problems of PERT," in P. Schoderbeek (Ed.), *Management Systems: A Book of Readings*. New York: John Wiley & Sons, 1967.

22. Stewart, R., "Management Education and Our Knowledge of Managers' Jobs," *International Social Science Journal*, XX, No. 1 (1968), pp. 77-89.

23. Stillan, G. S., "An Evaluation of PERT," in G. S. Stillan et. al., *PERT: A New Management Planning and Control Technique*. New York: American Management Association, 1962.

24. Stillan, G. S., et. al., *PERT: A New Management Planning and Control Technique*. New York: American Management Association, 1962.

25. USAF-PERT, Volume V, *Implementation Manual*, HG AFSC (SC CS), Washington, D. C.: Andrews Air Force Base, 1964.

26. Woodgate, H. S., *Planning by Network*. London, England: Business Publications, Ltd., 1964, Chapters 13 and 14.

Appendix
PERT Probability Aspects

One feature of PERT that distinguishes it from other management systems is the introduction of selected statistical concepts as an integral part of both the planning and controlling functions. While the statistical aspects have not been too widely employed in actual PERT implementation, an understanding of their purpose and nature will be useful to anyone intending to use the technique.

ACTIVITY TIME ESTIMATION

A basic PERT assumption is that the uncertainty associated with the time to complete an activity once started, is best represented by the Beta distribution. The mode of this distribution is at m (most likely time), with the range of estimates consisting of the interval between a (optimistic time estimate) and b (pessimistic time estimate).

An average or mean time to completion, called *The Expected Elapsed Time* and designated as t_e, is approximated for this distribution by use of the formula below.

$$t_e = \frac{a + 4m + b}{6}$$

This mean time is said to locate the 50 percent probability point of the Beta distribution as shown below. That is, there is a 50 percent chance that the actual time span will prove to be longer or shorter than the average time, or t_e.

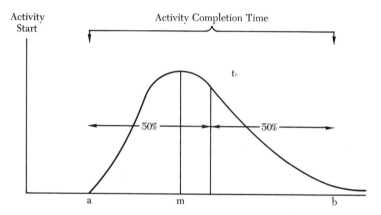

The standard deviation of the distribution is said to be approximated by the use of the formula below.

$$\sigma = \frac{b - a}{6}$$

The obtained standard deviation reflects the range of uncertainty associated with the time estimates for activity completion. Under this assumption, the optimistic and pessimistic time estimates are said to have a probability of .01 of being reached and therefore represent points located at three standard deviations plus or minus from the mean.

PROBABILITY OF MEETING A SCHEDULED OR DIRECTED DATE

Once an event is scheduled, a probability statement of meeting that schedule date can be obtained by using the previously obtained activity standard deviations. The procedural steps are outlined below.

For the particular event in question, the standard deviations are squared and then summed along the most critical path leading to the event. The square root of this sum is then obtained. The resulting statistic is said to represent the standard deviation of a distribution of T_E's (Earliest Expected Dates) for the specified event. This assumption is derived by using *The Central Limit Theorem*. The event standard deviation reflects the possibility that the event might be reached earlier or later than the calculated T_E date. The distribution of these dates is assumed to take the form of the normal distribution. The mean of the distribution is set at the T_E for the event in question as shown in the illustration below.

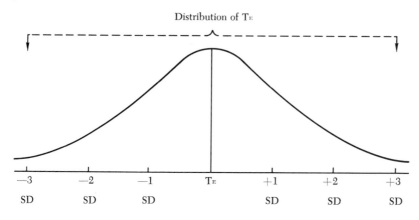

Distribution of T_E

To secure the probability statement, the formula for the normal deviate z is employed with appropriate substitutions as indicated in the formula below

$$z = \frac{T_S - T_E}{S_{T_E}}$$

where T_S equals the scheduled (or directed date) for the event, T_E is the events Earliest Expected date, and S_{T_E} is the event's standard deviation. Once the z is calculated, probability is secured by entering the normal distribution table and reading the accompanying percentage, adding to or subtracting from 50 percent depending on whether or not the z is positive or negative.

Example:

Given:
$$T_S = 12 \text{ weeks}$$
$$T_E = 10 \text{ weeks}$$

$$1 \; \frac{4 \underline{\hphantom{x}} 6 \underline{\hphantom{x}} 12}{S^2 = 1.17} \qquad 2 \; \frac{1 \underline{\hphantom{x}} 2 \underline{\hphantom{x}} 4}{S^2 = .50} \qquad 3$$
$$0.00 \qquad\qquad 1.77 \qquad\qquad 2.27$$

Variance Sums:

$$S_{T_E} = \sqrt{1.77 + .50} = \sqrt{2.27} = 1.51$$
$$= \frac{12 \underline{\hphantom{x}} 10}{1.51} = \frac{2}{1.51} = 1.32$$

Author Index

Subject Index

UM-5